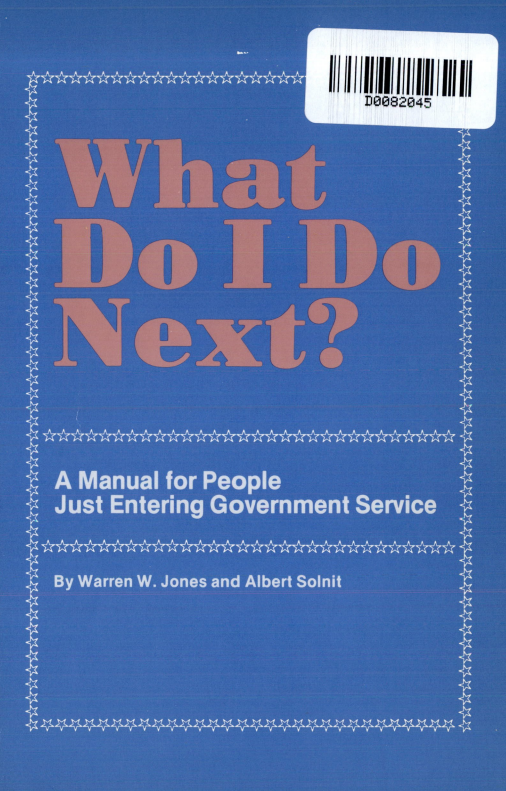

What Do I Do Next?

A Manual for People Just Entering Government Service

By Warren W. Jones and Albert Solnit

What Do I Do Next?

**A Manual for People
Just Entering Government Service**

What Do I Do Next?

A Manual for People Just Entering Government Service

**Warren W. Jones
and
Albert Solnit**

Cartoons by Richard Hedman

Planners Press
American Planning Association
Washington, D.C.   Chicago, Illinois

ISBN 0-918286-20-4

Library of Congress Catalog Card Number 80-67754

Printed in the United States of America

Table of Contents

Preface

Public service workers are facing uncertain and challenging times. A lot of work needs to be done, the agenda is long, and the public for whom they work is restless and demanding. This is true and will continue to be so. The issues on the public's agenda are difficult, and there are no easy solutions. The public no longer will tolerate final decisions made by the experts alone or decisions made in a vacuum without public participation. Both the public and the policymakers are demanding accountability, more and/or less government depending upon ideological and other factors, as well as more services without higher costs.

How is the new person in community development, public administration, local government, budgeting, housing, social services, or planning supposed to approach his or her job; be productive, fulfilled, and creative; survive in an increasingly politicized environment; and climb the career ladder in the midst of these conflicting public expectations? Remedies are needed, but this is not what this book is about.

This book is concerned with working in public service and ways to effectively cope with the demands of the public work place. Working in public service is different than working in the business world. While there are many books that deal with how to get, keep, and succeed in a job in business, virtually none has dealt with the unique nature of work in the public sector. These differences can be summed up as follows:

1. Public agencies deal with constituencies rather than markets. Thus the relationship between public servants and their "public" is much more complex than the buyer-seller transactions of the marketplace. While the vendor of automotive products can focus on how to persuade the public to buy a single product, the public official will be involved with provision and maintenance of a road system for automobile users, terminal facilities for shippers and shoppers, the provision and support of public transit for the nonautomobile owners, and also will be charged with carry-

ing out policies designed to reduce automobile travel in order to conserve energy, reduce pollution, and lessen congestion. Often the public official's mission is not only abstract, but controversial because there are winners and losers as a result of the implementation of any policy. These trade-offs and spill-over costs are central to the politics of hammering out public policy and need to be better understood by professionals who enter government service.

2. The public official deals in goods and services where the people who decide to spend money for them are not necessarily the ones who pay for them. In fact, in many cases, such as health, education, welfare, and public transit, the people that benefit are not the same people that pay the costs.

3. The standards for good performance on a public service job are often different than the ones in force in a private firm, but they are also much less discernable to the newcomer. This poses a dilemma for the newly hired person. *Who is my most important client?* "The people who make the rules and policies I implement, the public whose welfare I protect by applying the rules, the interests (often politically potent) I regulate, or the insiders in government over me who will rule on my raises and promotions?" It is obvious that this newcomer to public service is going to have to have special and unique skills in communication, judgment, diplomacy, and political awareness that the corporate executive can survive without.

4. The environment of the work place is very different in government. Strict accountability is required for every penny spent from public funds. Expense accounts, petty cash drawers, company lodges and yachts, posh offices, tax deductable travel, and other perks of the corporate executive life are conspicuously absent from the typical agency operation. An untax-sheltered salary is about all one can expect. Fame and recognition are

much harder to come by. Trips to tropical isles for star performers are rare, with few plaques and gold watches received at retirement. People in government service generally find it wise to keep low profiles. Pithy comments to the press and long-range wisdom and policy statements in front of an audience are the province of the mayor, council members, and supervisors. People who acquire survival instincts in public life learn early in their careers not to upstage their political employers in public affairs.

5. Pride of authorship usually has to be sublimated to fitting your piece of work into a style and format that goes well with other contributors. Your precious prose in letters and position papers will be drafted and revised for the style and signature of a superior. You will often have to support rules, policies, decisions, and procedures you don't fully agree with. Team players, rather than stars, are more highly prized in most agencies. In some places, your greatest attribute may be keeping the enemy out of the boss's hair. New people often have to serve as buffers or ''flak catchers'' for the senior people who have weightier things to do, as opposed to handling complaints and threats from all comers.

6. Public agencies generally harbor more deadwood than a cost-conscious firm. Thus a new person may have to strain against bottlenecks and foul-ups created by senior people with low productivity and even less interest in your problems. This situation was supposed to be

alleviated by the increasing scarcity of public funds, taxpayer revolts, and changes in the rules that truly overprotected the incompetent. However, in many jurisdictions, budget cuts meant that new, and often minority, rather than tired blood was shed by staff reductions.

7. Evaluation procedures for public employees during their probation periods have become more critical and, therefore, more hazardous to those who don't get off on the right foot from the start. Coupled with growing slashes in grants, increased costs for such benefits as health plans, social security, and so on, and the advent of zero-based budgeting, the job security one traditionally traded for the greater financial rewards of private enterprise is less present in public employment than ever before. Therefore, it is not going to be enough to be the best applicant for a job in government. More and more, the public service worker will have to demonstrate that he or she has the skills and ability to justify the continued existence of a place in the budget before the eyes of cost-cutting administrators and politicians.

The priorities of this book, then are to help you get, keep, and advance in your job in public service despite the changing nature of the work place. What we attempt to do first is help entry-level employees in public and quasi-public agencies understand the special characteristics of the many clients for whom they work and to understand the work place itself and the uniqueness of government service. Second, after reading this book, you should better understand the essential skills and capabilities you will need to survive. Third, each reader is encouraged to develop an appropriate career plan and a program to implement that plan. Finally, we have included a number of hints on job searching, resume writing, interviews, getting promoted, being listened to, asserting yourself, surviving in bureaucracies, and ultimately quitting with honor.

The material in this book is primarily aimed at people entering or who have just entered employment in an agency or firm that serves the public. But it should also serve many already on the job who are employed in planning, management, and program development or implementation. The same guidelines apply whether you are working for the state of Indiana, New York City, Crested Butte, Colorado, or Deaf Smith County, Texas. The professions represented may be public administration, urban planning, law, accounting, forestry, housing, finance, transportation, engineering, or health care, to name but a few.

The experience each person has on the first real job is not unlike the experience everyone else already has had. The new employee is uncertain and often insecure. The ways of the work place do not resemble the ways of academia: how an agency functions, office politics, professionalism, ethics, and career planning were not a part of the college curriculum. In short, few of us are equipped in advance to work in a public agency. We were provided with "generalist skills" (usually the result of a liberal education) and perhaps some very essential and useful specialist skills. Some already knew they would be most comfortable in a technician's role, and others wanted to be more active, perhaps even political. But we are shy on experience, mere beginners in social-personal, communication, program development, and management skills. And we rarely know anything about office politics, surviving in the bureaucracy, or the reasons why things are done the way they are, which at times is contrary to our expectations, values, or ethical standards.

These skills must be learned on the job. However, often there may not be time to learn. To help you become familiar with what has to be applied on the job is the main function of this book. The authors hope it will expedite the on-the-job learning process.

The authors also hope that the readers will use this book for self-evaluation and will become mindful of the possibilities of growth and change and will realize their true potential in the abstraction known as government.

Some would term all of this "finding the truth of your karma." Karma is the Zen doctrine that change is constant and according to a pattern, while all fixed forms, such as organization tables and job descriptions, are but appearances.

The ideal of a good career and of your life resembles a good piece of music in that the musician selects a piece that fits him because it brings out the full potential of his musicianship. Such music is a great work of art because it is simple; it is a unity whose full potential has been expressed. Your job in government should resemble the musician's music. It should be right, it should be unified with who you are, and it should change in harmony with the constant flux that is altering who you are and what you can do. "For the truly enlightened man subjection to the law of cause and effect and freedom from it are but one truth."[1]

As you proceed through this book, the authors hope you will understand one of our chief themes: that succeeding, helping others, having fun with your job, and effectiveness are all part of the process of personal development and growth, as well as what having a career is all about.

[1]Philip Kapleau, *The Wheel of Death* (New York: Harper & Row, 1971).

How to match up your skills with your own needs as well as with the expectations of your employer and the public—this is a tough job. It is hoped this book will help you find this path.

Chapter One
Changing Public Service
to Meet Changing
Public Values

> *All is flux. All is flow, constantly
> changing, changing . . .
> changing. . .*
>
> *Everything without exception is imperm-
> anent. . .Everything endlessly alters.*
>
> —Goenka, Buddist Teacher

Once upon a time, people looked to government to win their wars, solve their economic problems, protect their property, and do whatever private enterprise couldn't or didn't find it profitable to do. Government employees were accepted as useful citizens, just as the butcher, the baker, and the candlestickmaker. In fact, as recently as the 1960s, a widely held public belief existed that government was the mechanism whose magic and money would defeat poverty, restore life to the cities, save the environment, and cure any number of other defects of our soon-to-be "Great Society."

When many of us entered government service for the first time in those halcyon days, it was often as crusaders in a good cause. Then disillusionment set in. The guns of Viet Nam turned the Great Society's butter rancid. Then came Watergate—the final "breach of trust" in government leadership and rhetoric. Today, the person who chooses a career in government does not enjoy the halo effect of high hopes and ambitious programs with large budgets.

Today, the challenge takes the form of constantly justifying the existence of your agency and your job to skeptical elected officials who more and more reflect the disillusioned taxpayers—taxpayers beset by inflation which lowers their real income and by a change in attitude about how big government should be and how much it should do. For more and more citizens, government is already too big and does too much. This means that the person entering government will have to find a new style for the rest of the country.

Moreover, this person is going to be challenged as never before. Despite the storm of political rhetoric, Americans are looking to their government to do something constructive about the serious problems of energy shortages, environmental degradation, the slumping economy, decaying cities, and a whole host of other problems. For people who want to add their efforts to the amount of work that needs to be done in these areas, as well as working to maintain the general welfare, raise the quality of life, and see that social justice is done, public service is the only place where it is happening. Special psychic rewards and lasting achievements flow from a job well done in public service that are unobtainable in the higher-paying jobs in private enterprise. Nevertheless public attitudes toward government and the people who work there have shifted towards greater and greater antipathy. The person entering government service in the 80s will have to contend with the following glittering generalizations being given currency by the media, aspiring candidates for political office, syndicated satirists, and even college professors, who are a species of bureaucrat themselves:

1. Government organizations are bumbling inefficient systems run by remote bureaucrats, who've insulated themselves from the public they should be serving by establishment of a baffling maze of rules, procedures, and self-serving paperwork, which foster delay and complexity at the expense of useful products and timely results.[1]

2. Government goods and services are not subject to the same standards of value as private goods and services, so that taxpayers can be easily fooled about whether or not they are getting "value" in proportion to their cost. Moreover, economists cannot offer much help on establishing the value in dollars of clean air, protection of an endangered species, holding land off the market for open space, subsidizing decent housing for the poor, and so on. All they can do is point to the cost, while the people in charge of government programs are often stuck with arguing value in terms of moral abstractions against the specific dollar amounts of costs.

3. Government, especially on the local level, is resistant to changes that would make it more efficient. For example the House Subcommittee on Cities after years of study concluded: "Local governments must

become more efficient. . .public employees perceive change as a threat to their jobs. So Model T governments bounce along half a century behind the times.''

4. There is too much government control over people's lives and free enterprise. Much of this charge is aimed at recent social and environmental legislation by special interest groups whose economic interests have been adversely affected by mandates to protect the environment and promote social goals. However, some examples of overly elaborate permit procedures and other red tape have been of immense help to the supporters of this position.

5. The American public is becoming increasingly tuned out to politics in general and government in particular. For example, The Committee for the Study of the American Electorate reported that only 37.9 percent of voting-age Americans cast ballots in the 1978 statewide elections. That marked the fourth successive decline of voting in a nonpresidential election year. Voter participation in the 1978 congressional elections was the lowest since 1942, only 35 percent of the eligible voters.

This trend seems to mean that the electorate is turning into a permanent nonparticipating majority. Thus the person who seeks to enlist broad public participation and support for a program, plan, or proposal will have to work harder than ever before and be even better at it. Of course, special interests and chronic aginners will always be with us. Easily available, unbiased representative citizens to serve on advisory committees and other participatory bodies may be as hard to find in many localities as a ten cent cup of coffee.

While public apathy and disenchantment with the governmental process have undoubtedly been on the increase, government will still remain a good place in which to make a career. It is much more than making a living for the dedicated and skilled graduate. It is working for a greater good than black ink in a corporate profit report. And it is community service where you can make a contribution to your city, nation, and society in ways that are often exciting and of lasting importance. Finally, government's role has not only been changing at an accelerating pace, but its role has grown more and more important, despite its detractors, because who else can tackle today's problems in all their sizes and complexity.

Nevertheless, for the person just entering government, the current mood of public apathy and distrust toward government in general and bureaucracy in particular poses a new challenge. You will need to justify the existence of your agency and your job in terms that people can understand and evaluate. Administrators, politicians, and citizens who do participate have increasingly been demanding that you prove that they are getting value for the money requested at budget time. All these circumstances point to the fact that people in government will have to look into their consciences and see if their service, motives, and skills are attuned to the new mood toward public employees and government itself.

This book will try to help you find out what to do next about your career, whether you're looking for your first job or trying to figure out what to do with the one you've got. One of the major objectives of this book is to try to help the entry-level professional in government to get off on the right foot and to advance in the right direction.

This means being more efficient in a lot of skills that were not highly valued in the public servant of the past. Many of these skills, such as clear writing and speaking, teamwork, concern for effective use of time, economical use of money, and other resources over which a public official has stewardship, are often not taught in schools of public policy, planning, and public administration and are often discouraged by the students' role models—the exaulted mandarins on the faculty.

This book, therefore, is aimed at helping students avoid, and recent graduates break, the bad habits instilled by "getting an education." Our objective is to help you get a job in the "real world" and develop your career as a public employee or adviser to public officials.

Now that the "real world" has gotten even more real for public job seekers, it is time to warn degree holders and job seekers that the following realities will be confronted on a daily basis:

1. Work will not be like term papers. You will not be able to coast until the last minute and then dash off a "literary gem" based on one-part plagiarism to two-parts rehash of your lecture notes. You will be expected to be productive everyday. Fortifying yourself with No Doze® to make it under the wire will not earn the rewards it did at school.

2. You're going to have to think on your feet, apply what you know to new situations, and learn to communicate simply with people who may not agree with you (and who surely won't understand the academic language.

3. You're going to be tested more frequently, without warning, so you will not be able to cram. These tests will not only be on the quality of your work, especially the results it gets, but how much you cost to turn it out. This not only means your time, but how effective were you in getting others—the typists, the draftsmen, the statisticians, the computer programmers—to work effectively under your direction on your project.

4. You must have some measurable skills to survive. Good intentions, those abstract notions of how things ought to be, are not enough. The people you work for will not buy rhetoric.

5. Perhaps up to half of your time will be spent learning how to get along with others, functioning in a team, dealing with office and real politics, figuring out workable strategies to make things happen, and persuading others to do something you think worthwhile.

6. You will be monitored for effectiveness, and not necessarily by your peers. For years, effectiveness was not as important a condition of employment as it is now becoming.

NOTES

1. The bureaucratic system of ponderous inertia has been summed up as follows: "The system is actually a way of life where decisions are approached in writing, step by measured step. . .Results are ground out at an unhurried pace, thus assuring everyone that any problem, plan, proposal, or plea—irrespective of cost or size—will receive exactly the same consideration. . .The Principle is upheld by seeing to it that each case to be striven over is stripped of its apparent simplicity and rearranged into the complexity it really is—or should be." John Kidner, *The Kidner Report* (Washington, D.C.; Acropolis Books, 1972), p. 26.

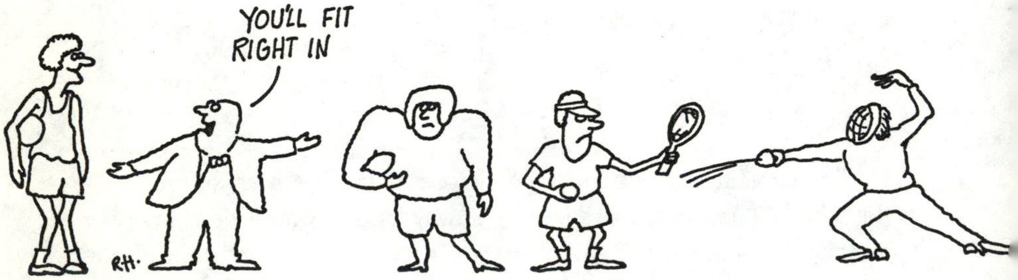
YOU'LL FIT RIGHT IN
RH.

Chapter Two
Getting Started on
the Right Foot

*Has any man ever attained inner
harmony by pondering the experience of
others?*

*Not since the world began! He must pass
through the fire.*

—Norman Douglas, *South Wind*

CHARACTERISTICS OF THE WORK PLACE

Who's Your Client? Everyone!

Now that you've finally got that job, you have to start learning what it really is. More than anything else, you must register positively with two different sets of people.

INSIDERS. These are the people inside the organization who will promote, evaluate, direct, and gossip about you. They include:
- Your department head.
- His or her administrators.
- Your immediate supervisor.
- Your co-workers.
- The support staff in the agency (clerical, purchasing, drafting, computer programming, and so on.)

OUTSIDERS. These are the people with whom you deal, serve, or contend with in carrying out your job responsibilities. They include, not necessarily in order of importance:
- The chief administrative officer of the jurisdiction.
- His or her administrative aids.
- Other department heads and their subordinates.

- Elected officials.
- Citizen boards and commissions.
- Special private interest groups and their representatives.
- The general public.

Who's important and who isn't on this list? One useful rule of thumb is to consider that anyone you depend on to get direction, get work done, or for performance evaluation is important and should be treated as such. For example, the department head's executive secretary may have more clout than your immediate supervisor in helping assess whether you are fitting into the organization adequately. And she (or he) may get much of her (or his) information about you from the typists you've treated badly when they didn't get your report ready on time. Perhaps the following insulating advice will help you pass through the probationary fire among all those strangers you will be working with.

Insiders

SUPPORT STAFF. Find out who gives them their work assignments and work with the system that prevails. Often it's cumbersome and inefficient, but the time for reform will come later when you are accepted

Figure 2.1. County Planning Department—Organization Chart

A typical and Still-too-Common Pyramid Which Usually Bogs Down
Into Freelance Anarchy and/or Static Chaos

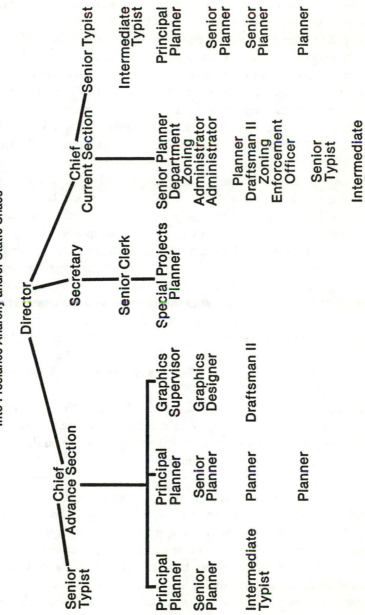

or want to issue a parting statement when you leave for greener pastures.[1] For example, in a county planning department where one of the authors worked, the reporting and work assignment system was chaotic (see Figure 2.1). The director's secretary did the department's purchasing, a job she not only loathed, but scarcely had time for. As a result, the things that were needed were only purchased after she got a direct order from the remote, hard-to-see director of the department. The situation was even worse in the graphics section, for the supervisor took on work assignments only after being instructed by the director, who being new to the job usually waffled about deadlines, changing them frequently without telling the section chiefs.

Situations such as this are quite common and often lead to conflict with the people who take orders from one group and then work for another. Be sympathetic to their plight. Don't assume that your work is as important to them as it is to you. If you have to work through their supervisor to get the work assignment placed, then go through channels. *Don't ever short cut lines of authority* with the support staff by just dumping a 173-page report on the typist's desk with a throwaway line such as, "We need a rough draft of this in two days for the meeting."

Work out informal arrangements based on mutual respect and trust with these people. For example:

1. Always write out what you want done: Is the report a draft or a final version? How many copies? When do you need it? Who gets the original? Copies? And so on.

2. Make your agreement on how and when by writing a memo on what you agreed to do. Ask to be notified immediately if something comes up to change this contract. Better yet, keep an eye on the progress others are making. Don't be caught by surprise.

3. When you are familiar with why the system was established the way it is, you might start to *tactfully* work to improve it. For example, the graphics supervisor insisted that no one talk directly to his men. He felt they "got to gabbing" with everyone who came up from the rest of the department, and then there was no way to guarantee that deadlines would be met. However, when he was taught to lay out a graphics job on a critical path, he realized that it was logical to schedule conferences between the report writer and the person who was responsible for the graphics. These took the form of checkpoints on the schedule. Once he realized that contact between his draftsmen and others was going to be structured and work related, he agreed to modify the top-down direction of the arrows and permit some lateral contact.

YOUR CO-WORKERS.   One of the hardest things for many people after they leave school is to become a team player. Any group that has a task to perform together has an internal agenda to cover first; namely, the group process, which is the creation and maintenance of the productive functioning of a group. Organization Dynamics, Inc., a management training firm, lists four major factors that are important in effective group functioning. These are especially important in working positively with your co-workers.

Support—behavior of one person toward another that increases the other's feelings of his [or her] own worth as a person.

Goal Emphasis—behavior of person that stimulates in another a genuine enthusiasm to achieve commonly shared goals.

Work Faciliation—behavior that helps another person accomplish more by removing obstacles to his or her performance.

Team Building—behavior between two (or more) persons that builds a closely knit cohesive interaction that accomplishes common goals with less effort.

Group Think.   Sometimes the group gets so cohesive that people in the group hesitate to speak critically, smooth over debate, avoid responsibility, rationalize their consensus (often forced) as being "morally right," and adopt a "we and they" attitude toward others not in the group. This kind of behavior gave the nation the Bay of Pigs, the prolongation of the Viet Nam war, and most of the crimes of Watergate. Remember that since you are in *public* service, a "we and they" attitude is fatal to doing a proper job.

Setting Up Shop.   Many organizations have people who've carved out their own little empires—set up shop—and will not cooperate on

anything that threatens their status quo whether it's changing "the way things have always been done" or "taking on new work." As John Kidner points out, "born bureaucrats must want things to conform to an established pattern to force a fit when they do not."[2]

Work teams or task forces of co-workers are often leaderless. While opinion is divided on whether it's really necessary to select a leader, individual roles are commonly taken by members of a work group. No one plays all these roles, nor does anyone usually play the same role all the time:

Task Roles
Initiating (tasks, goals, ideas, and so on).
Information or opinion seeking.
Clarifying (clearing confusions, giving examples, and so on).
Summarizing (pulling ideas together).
Consensus testing (checking for agreement).

Group Maintenance Roles
Harmonizing (reducing tension, getting people to explore differences).
Encouraging (giving positive strokes).
Expressing group feelings (sensing moods and relationships within the group).
Setting standards (expressing standards for the group to keep).
Compromising (suggesting means to resolve polarized positions on issues).
Gatekeeping (keeping everyone involved; usually a chairman's role).

Negative Roles which the group must police
Distractors (hair splitters, anecdote spinners, and so on).
Topic jumpers (people who don't stay on the subject).
Cynics (Gee, what can we do? It's no use trying, we'll only get overruled, and so on).
Continuous talkers.
Withdrawal.
Irrelevant horsing around (often masks contempt for the group task).
Manipulative games (using others for self-interest, oneupmanship).

YOUR IMMEDIATE SUPERVISOR.   It is vital to stay on the right side of your immediate supervisor, who will do the most critical evaluations of your performance. Doing good work is necessary; however, most people are discharged because of character traits rather than a lack of skills. A survey of office workers found that 89.9 percent of discharges were based on character trait deficiencies.[3] Heading the list were carelessness (14.1 percent), noncooperation (10.7 percent), laziness (10.3 percent), absence for causes other than illness (8.5 percent), dishonesty (8.1 percent), (too much) attention to outside things (7.9 percent), lack of initiative (7.6 percent) and lack of ambition (7.2 percent). While government agencies cannot fire with the ease of corporations, transfers-which-equal banishment, lack of promotion, and other more subtle forms of dehiring do exist for handling people who have these deficiencies.

It is very hard to know how to register positively with a boss without toadying. Peter Drucker said:

> Recognize that the boss is neither a monster nor an angel, he's a human being who insists on behaving like one. . .For some bosses, you polish the apple: for others it's the worst thing you can do. . .No matter how able and competent the boss is, he is not a mind reader. You have to make sure he understands what you're trying to do. . .With some bosses, you tell them exactly what you're going to do; others, you ask for their advice. It depends on how the boss works, not on what you like.[4]

"The Radovic Rule" is a tongue-in-cheek response to the conventional wisdom on how to manage your superior. Radovic counsels:

> a. In any organization, the potential is much greater for the subordinate to manage his superior than for the superior to manage his subordinate.
> b. The maximum rewards in employment are not to be found in upward mobility but in stability at the rank and file level.
> c. The less inviting or more repugnant a job appears to be to the initiated, the more irreplaceable the subordinate doing it will be considered, and the more independence and job satisfaction he can win for himself.[5]

The Radovic Rule does work, especially in large organizations. One large county community development department kept a very limited person around for years at a section chief's salary, because he had taken over the street naming and numbering process. Developers courted his favor more than they did the planning director, because he could confer immortality by having sole power to approve proposals for Boleslovsky Boulevards and Connie-Jo Lanes.

YOUR DEPARTMENT HEAD. If your department head is not your immediate supervisor as well, he or she will probably be remote. You will only be visable on such ceremonial occasions as staff meetings, budget sessions and departmental presentations at public meetings, or at the annual Christmas party.

Meetings where the No. 1 is present can be very dangerous to novices. Very often novices will find themselves backed into a tight corner when asked a question or when they meet unexpected opposition to something they said.

Dennis James suggests two ways to emerge safely.

1. *Be Frankly Ignorant*
If you find it difficult to ad lib try the frank admission of ignorance, sometimes known as snivelling. Apologetically you say, "Mr. Chairman

[usually the director or his administrator], I'm afraid you've caught me out, I just don't have those figures with me. Please leave this matter with me and I will deal with it after the meeting.''

The chairman is delighted to have caught someone on the hop and forced him to admit it. The rest of the meeting he will have only a vague recollection of the conversation because [everyone was] busy studying [other matters] so the point is passed over.

2. *The Technique of Ready Response* known as TORR (paraphrased for a government situation)

Question: ''Jim, can you tell me why that report on geologic hazards and ground water is not ready yet?''

Jim (who was mentally reliving his two weeks at Acapulco last winter) comes to earth with a jerk and says without a moments hesitation: ''The test boring rig has had trouble with the reverse tension hydraulic former and has had to go back to the service center people who are very slow at getting parts from the Hong Kong factory!''

This is the important part of TORR—a quick authoritative answer straight out of the box. The meeting proceeds (and Jim can check his facts afterwards). If, as is almost certain, he is wrong, he can ask the minutes to be changed at the next meeting, implying rather logically that he was misquoted.[6]

More seriously, novices need to know their places. Despite the rhetoric, most work places are not egalitarian democracies. Points to keep in mind for getting on with the department heads are:

- Managers give opinions, employees give advice, and the real boss takes notes and decides later.
- Don't speak at meetings unless you have something to say. Don't use the department head's time unless it's absolutely necessary.
- If you want the department head to set your project in motion, get the background work done and have it ready for his or her okay or signature in the form of a finished letter, resolution, agenda, and so on.
- You can cross the chain of command with communication of an advisory nature, but never with orders.

DEPARTMENT ADMINISTRATORS. Charged with trying to keep the agency machinery working, department administrators are often responsible for evaluating your performance and for making salary and promotion recommendations to the department head. Getting answers for the following questions are generally necessary to evaluate a new or probationary employee. Administrators do this not only by interviewing everyone in contact with you, but keeping track of complaints, foul-ups, and so on in your file.

1. *Volume of acceptable work completed.* Do you consistently accomplish a day's work for a day's pay?
2. *Meeting deadlines.* Do you make an honest attempt to meet deadlines and give advance notice when you can't?
3. *Job skill level.* Do you consistently demonstrate the skills prerequisite to the job description and standards? Is the work accurate or does it have to be redone?
4. *Oral and written expression.* Do you have the ability to communicate effectively with fellow workers and the public?
5. *Attendance and reliability in work hours.* Are you getting famous for long lunches, field trips, late arrivals, and missed meetings and appointments?
6. *Taking direction.* Do you constantly whine and bicker about job assignments or accept faulty instructions passively without a full understanding of what you're supposed to do?
7. *Planning and organization.* Do you plan and organize the steps on an assigned job to achieve the required results? Or do you attack the work thoughtlessly or with such blind enthusiasm that mistakes occur and deadlines are missed?
8. *How you get along with others.* Are you a disruptive influence? Do you lower the morale of your co-workers by constant griping? Do you bother them with your personal problems, and so on?
9. *Meeting and handling the public.* Does your contact with the public through personal or telephone conversation, correspondence, and day-to-day public appearances promote a good image of the agency or jurisdiction you represent?
10. *Performance in new situations.* Do you accept change willingly or slow it down by resistance and lack of flexibility?
11. *Performance under stress.* Can you work effectively in situations where pace, pressure, and tempo are demanding? Can you respond productively in an emergency?

Outsiders

Outsiders judge you on how well you present yourself. The characteristics of presentation differ according to which type of group you are addressing.

CITIZEN GROUPS. Most of the time these meetings are held to present information and elicit feedback. Since the main purpose of these meetings are for the sake of communication, they should be open and reasonably well structured so everyone present will be able to speak without hindrance.

General Interest Group. This group is frequently made up of civic-minded homemakers and senior citizens. This group is rarely effective as a counter-pressure group when issues are being decided at the political level. However, it does provide the citizen participation that many projects and programs must have.

Local Interest Group. Such groups generally coalesce around a single issue such as a threat to the neighborhood (proposed new project, hazardous intersection, crime, and so on). They are often "aginners" in that they want something or some condition stopped, and in wealtheir areas, they are increasingly represented by a "hired gun" attorney. They can get out of hand, if not carefully handled, especially if they think the staff person isn't in agreement with them. It's important to have such meetings chaired and controlled by someone they respect. Either the chairman of their own organization or a heavyweight politican (member of the city council or congress or so on) should buffer and intercept the latent hostility, or the meeting can degenerate into a shouting match. The buffer person should announce what the meeting is for, give the ground rules for speaking, and tell who you are and what you've got to do with giving them what they want. If you're only there for fact-finding, exploration, or alternatives and to listen, this should be pointed out, so you won't get the pressure that they've been saving for the politicians. Be very careful: be able to back up everything you say. Don't voice opinions, or try to wing it during the question-and-answer period.

Local Organizations. Organizations such as the neighborhood associations, homeowners or landowner's council, and so on are frequently knowledgeable about dealing with government agencies, have a long history of doing so, and know their power to influence decisions. They usually have direct access to their city councilmembers or county commissioners. Often their district politician will also be their advocate on issues which affect them. You are, therefore, acting more as a diplomatic emissary from government. If you goof in someway, people at the top will hear about it directly, and retribution will magnify as it filters down to you. Therefore, it's important to do your homework carefully on what your specific mission is (for example, communicate information or agency policy (with or without interpretation) or get response to options, priorities, objectives, or whatever.) Have some idea from your superior as to what the results of a successful meeting should be. Being diplomatic means never having to say you're sorry.

Citizens Advisory Committee. Generally, this is a task force, often blue ribbon, focused on a single product such as a budget, a plan, or a program. The committee is usually charged with studying and reporting to the appointing body on what members think should be done about the topic studied. Your need is to serve as temporary staff, often in liaison with a consultant or people from another agency to prepare findings and recommendations in the form of a report. Careful listening, facilitating clear opinions, and getting things down in language designed to capture the feeling of what was said are the important skills needed.

SPECIAL INTEREST ORGANIZATIONS. Such groups as the chamber of commerce, union representatives, Sierra Club members, or groups of farmers or builders represent a sort of protective association for the benefit of their members. Thus, they take stands on whether or not a proposal is good or bad from their particular prospective. For example, the construction unions may be on strike against the builders, but they will still team up to support a big (whether bad or good) project at public hearings on the basis that this project will provide more jobs.

Often there is an anti-special interest group involved in the same issue, so someone looking for middle ground can get caught in the cross fire (for example, minority organizations who are pro low-cost housing and jobs versus environmental groups who want to slow down growth, keep many developable areas open, and so on). Often these groups have their own staff and fact-finding capabilities and woe betide the governmental person who presents sloppy or inaccurate work.

For example, at a presentation during a public hearing in support of a controlled-growth program, the staff of a county planning department pointed out that all the new homes with an average of four persons per household would soon swamp the roads, schools, and other public facilities. The developer's staff then pointed out that the planner's arithmetic was incorrect and that current figures showed only slightly more than two persons per household in new single family homes and less than two in apartments and mobile homes. Their credibility destroyed,

Figure 2.2. Handy Guide to Public Policy Proposers and Their Proposals

General Guidelines for Post-Industrial Citizenship: (1) pick up any position or combination thereof; (2) don't look at other policy proposals—you are right.

Ideological Positions	View of Present and Future	Proposals for Future
1. Horrified Humanist	A slim chance of surviving our chaos and obsolescence	Sweeping reforms, world government, national planning
2. Languishing Liberal	Troubled times	More money and programs, racial integration
3. Middling Moderate	No thoughts; cross-pressured	Various platitudes to avoid offending other policy proposers
4. Counteracting Conservative	Crime, centralization, and crumbling civilization	Law, order, soap, haircuts, Truth and Morality
5. Rabid Rightist	It's getting REDder all the time	Wave flags and stockpile arms (public and private)
6. Primitive Populist	Domination by pointy-headed pseudo-intellectuals	Throw briefcases in Potomac, restore common sense
7. Passionate Pacifist	A garrison state	A peaceable kingdom
8. Radical Romantic	A cancered civilization	Small experimental communities
9. Rumbling Revolutionary	A repressive, racist, imperialist, capitalist establishment	Confront and destroy The System (other details worked out later)
10. Apocalyptic Apostle	Armageddon coming to a sinful world	Be saved

Role-Related Positions

1. Urgent Urbanist	Decline and fall of cities	More funds and programs sidestepping states
2. Emphatic Ecologist	Decline and fall of everything else	Control contaminators and restore nature
3. Boiling Blackman	Here a pig, there a pig, everywhere a pig pig	Black everything
4. Status-Seeking Sibling Sender	Crisis in our schools and colleges	More funds and programs, tax deductions
5. Multi-Megamuscled Militarist	Growing Chinese and/or Russian capabilities	More National Security regardless of national security
6. Technocrat-on-the-Take	No thoughts: not within scope of specialty	Well-funded studies and use of areane models
7. Sincerely Sorry Scientist	Profligate technology	Think of alternative futures and their consequences
8. Bullied Budget-Binder	Up-tight	Making this year's budget and getting more for next year
9. Tortured Taxpayer	Growing gaps between income, aspirations, and expenditures	Cut, cut, cut, cut, cut, cut
10. Stultified Student	Entrapment in *their* world	Inner and interpersonal exploration, and other relevant learning
11. Contracting	Cybernation, diversifica-	Withering of the state

Conglomerator	tion, and internation-alization	
12. Hi-throttle Highwayman	Paving the nation	Re-paving the nation
13. Frustrated Feminist	Futility, frivolity, and frigidaires	Fun-filled fulfillment
14. Star-Struck Spaceman	Up, up, and away	Science must not be impeded
15. Bonded Bureaucrat	Six years to retirement	Longer coffee breaks

Source: Figure by Michael Marien. Reprinted from *Public Administration Review*, March-April 1970, p. 154. Copyright 1970 by The American Society for Public Administration, 1225 Connecticut Ave. NW, Washington, DC 20036. All rights reserved.

the county planners were sent back to the drawing board and the growth-control program was scuttled.

Such special interest organizations often take a rigid ideological position. Since such positions are not debatable, the novice in government should never be lured into such debate—especially on home ground (see Figure 2.2).

GOVERNMENT CLIENTS

Elected Officials. Because these people usually have only a very limited time to spend on many of the things that come before them, they usually have only a hazy grasp of the details of the issues. Therefore, they will use their heads for what they know best—assessing the political pros and cons of the issue—and will tend to hold the rational, objective recommendations of technical people at arms length. Meetings are formal, structured, and legalistic. Political advisors or aides work under great handicaps. Agendas are usually overfull, meetings and hearings inevitably run later than scheduled, more people want to speak than time allows, and so the young staff person who has rehearsed a brilliant 20-minute presentation with maps, charts, tables, and written reports, often finds he or she is to get the message across in the three minutes before bids for a park concession are opened. (It's natural to think what you've labored on for months is the most important matter on the agenda; elected officials may not, particularly if it's a "bad news" item that's likely to cause more political grief than joy.) People who stumble and fumble when asked to edit their presentations down to a summary on a moment's notice are remembered, usually at budget time when cuts are proposed.

Another trap to avoid while standing before politicians in their august chambers is going in with only one option, especially on a controversial matter. Often staff people's recommendations are used as foils by politicians in structuring more politically appealing compromises, so that the technician gets caught in the middle and comes off looking unreasonable and rigid, while the politicians appear to be humane and diplomatic. But if you keep your options at the ready, you won't be frozen out of compromise decisions. Another good piece of advice was given this writer by his first city manager: "Don't buy the problem. Let others work on the solution, too. After all, it's boring to see someone constantly trying to prove he's got a hammerlock on truth."

Boards and Commissioners.   Many boards and commissioners are ill equipped to handle their jobs because of lack of training, orientation, and experience. If you are a staff person to such a body, it's important not to become their guru. Keeping these lay members in a dependency state may boost your ego, but it's bad for the public interest because you are not supposed to do their job for them. What they bring to the decision- and policymaking process is their sense of values. For example, will this proposal be of benefit to all the citizens of the community? Your judgment should not be substituted for theirs at this level. As with the citizens advisory committee, your staff role is to facilitate their sending up reasoned, fact-based recommendations to their parent body. You should act as educator, data gatherer, issue interpreter, plus sounding board for the technical feasibility of their issues.

Other Department Heads and Their Subordinates.   These individuals are often found on interagency councils, technical advisory committees, and other special committees, where the dynamics can usually be described as "where one stands depends on where one sits." Many will be messengers who cannot bend their house rules or policies. They are just there to absorb what's going on and report back.

Occasionally you will seek the cooperation of a decisionmaker from a foreign department or agency. Perhaps your department needs some matching services for a federal grant or a review of an environmental impact statement by a certain date. In this instance, you are conducting diplomatic negotiations with a sovereign entity. You need to know what is important to that entity—what is their standard operating procedure and where they're coming from. You need to have a good argument to prove why they would benefit from taking on new work, how much authority goes with any responsibility (can they write a minority report, where does their name appear on the cover of the report, and so on). It is best to cultivate a friend in such outside entities, whom you can contact on an informal basis, and who can "bird dog" information sources, set up appointments, feed you inside intelligence, and so on.

Finally, remember no one will willingly submit to being coordinated. Have an ample supply of carrots and sticks before attempting this most difficult feat of intergovernmental art and skill.

Chief Administrative Officers and Their Aids. Since their interest in you will probably be to assess you as fodder for the next round of budget cuts, do not present yourself to them during a probationary period. Follow this rule instead: *In obscurity is security.*

JOB ROLES AND YOU

Roles and Responsibilities in Government Service

In government service, there are ten roles to play or ten functions to perform. You might play one or two in a career, or all of them; that is a matter of personal choice.

EXECUTIVE MANAGER. Examples of this top-level position might be the city or county manager or the director of a regional transportation agency. Usually this person has an identifiable set of management and political skills as well as experience in many other areas of competence.

ADMINISTRATIVE AIDE. Examples might be the assistant city manager or the deputy director. Much of their work is once removed from the political arena and is closer to the internal workings of the agency.

FUNCTIONAL MANAGER OR ADMINISTRATOR. The chief of police, director of community development, and chief of advance planning in the planning department are examples of this level of government. This person is in charge of a special area or function and not the entire agency. However, the job requires management and coordinative skills as well as specialist skills.

PROGRAM DESIGNER. Urban planners, policy analysts, engineers, anti crime specialists, and health care planners are specialists, who know how to identify problems, survey the needs of clients, and design overall programs that chart out how things are going to get done and by whom. They are instrumental in keeping policy advisers and helping policymakers adopt policies, plans, rules, and regulations.

PHYSICAL DESIGNER. Other specialists in urban planning, urban design, and engineering may be equipped to put ideas and programs to paper and to lay out workable design solutions, such as plans for street widenings, for a new waste water treatment system, or for renewing a town square or creating a pedestrian mall.

PROGRAM AND PLAN REVIEWER. The personnel in the current planning section of city and county planning departments judge the proposals of others to determine conformity with established policies and regulations. They do not make the rules; they apply them.

REGULATOR OR ENFORCER. Building and housing officials, zoning administrators, police and fire personnel are true specialists whose well-focused responsibilities are usually narrowly defined. For the most part, they carry out and enforce the rules prepared and agreed to by others.

POLICY AND PROGRAM IMPLEMENTATOR. Personnel in planning, redevelopment, and recreation take public programs that spell out agreed upon public policies and initiate public action. They assume the responsibility for implementing policies and programs through actions, such as land purchase, housing finance, land clearance, publicly sponsored park improvements, or publicly funded health care activities.

POLICY AND PROGRAM EVALUATOR. Some staff members or consultants systematically examine and evaluate policies, programs, and actions to determine if they are adequate and well administered or, perhaps, inappropriate and ill managed.

ADVOCATE. Other staff members facilitate group processes within the community, engage in organizational development, assist neighborhood groups, and help out-of-power or under-represented groups to create an affective and sustained power base.

Deciding What Role Is Right for You

As a job seeker or individual starting up the career ladder, you will be looking for a position in one of these categories. At the beginning, you cannot expect to qualify for an executive management or administrative position, but the other categories are real possibilities. In some agencies, you might fit into more than one role and be expected to. In others, you may become a specialist with little room for horizontal movement. In all cases, experience on the first job is the critical proving ground for learning more about yourself and deciding what you do well, cannot stand doing, or want to do next.

Certain attributes and skills are called for in each category. Many are transferable. Later you will have an opportunity to renew your own background, abilities, and skills, and to consider where you might fit. But to do this, you need to identify the attributes and skills needed to perform effectively in each of the ten job roles (see Figure 2.3).

NOTES

1. A witty British friend stated, "One should treat an awkward new job situation like a temporary love affair. Enjoy what you have embraced in the full knowledge that you'll be getting up to go on to better things soon."

2. John Kidner, *The Kidner Report* (Washington, D.C.: Acropolis Books, 1972), p. 19.

3. Paul W. Boynton, *So You Want a Better Job* (New York: Socony Vacuum Oil Company, 1947).

4. "How to Boss the Boss—and Succeed," *San Francisco Chronicle,* June 8, 1977.

5. Igor Radovic, *How to Manage the Boss: The Radovic Rule* (New York, M. Evans, 1973), pp. vi, vii, and 31.

6. Dennis James, *Bluff Your Way in Management* (London: Wolfe Publishing Ltd., 1969). pp. 13-14.

Figure 2.3. Attributes and Skills Needed to Perform Adequately

Job Role	Responsibilities	Attributes Needed	Minimum Skills Needed*
Executive Manager	Manages and administers an agency Reports to and is responsible to an elected body Represents the agency before the public Has fiscal responsibility	Political savy Patience Ability to balance assertive style with the need to compromise A sense of mission	Generalist skills Some job-relevant specialist skills Awareness of appropriate new technology skills All of the social-personal skills All of the communication skills All of the work programming and management skills Well-polished stylistic skills
Administrative Aide	Assists in managing and administering an agency Reports to and is responsible to the chief executive Communicates the executive's program and orders to staff May have certain specified functional duties and oversee the work of others in the hierarchy	Loyalty to the chief executive Ability to understudy the chief executive and to serve in the capacity if required	All of the above, with full recognition that as understudy you are gaining more and more experience over time
Functional Manager or Administrator	Is responsible to the chief executive or assistant for carrying out specified functional duties, administering staff, and managing a budget	Ability to work as a member of a team toward common objectives Productive; results-oriented	Given that this is a management position, in effect, all of the above, proportional to the needs of the job
Program Designer	Prepares overall program designs for specified needs Prepares specific work programs and implementation strategies	Ability to think systematically and creatively Well-organized approach to problem	Generalist skills Appropriate specialist skills Appropriate new technology skills Appropriate social-personal, communication, and

	given needs Manipulates concepts and policies within a physical setting or space Prepares maps, drawings, plans, and graphic displays	Communicates graphically	skills Appropriate communication skills Work programming skills
Program and Plan Reviewer	Reviews proposals of others and judges their suitability against existing rules, policies, regulations, and guidelines Recommends approval or denial, or conditions of approval	Understands not only the rules but the reasons behind them and is able to explain them to others Ability to apply rules in in accordance with legal legal due process	Appropriate specialist skills, social-personal, and communication skills
Regulator or Enforcer	Regulates and enforces the rules (policies, regulations, standards, conditions, guidelines) of the public agency, as necessary or required	Ability to apply the rules in accordance with legal due process Discrete, fair, even handed, and incorruptible	Appropriate social-personal and communications skills Stylistic skills
Policy and Program Implementor	Takes policies and overall program outlines and figures out how to get things done Assumes responsibility for getting action through a variety of means	Action-oriented Prides self in getting things done Budget and time conscious Innovative	Appropriate specialist and new technology skills Appropriate social-personal, communications skills Some work programming and management skills
Policy and Program Evaluator	Examines and evaluates in-place programs according to pre-determined criteria and judges (and reports on) their effectiveness	Analytic	Appropriate specialist skills
Advocate	Tries to speak and act on behalf of others, especially the less advantaged	Spiritual or conceptual concern for those out of power or disadvantaged Ability to walk the tightrope between government policy (and styles) and needs of others Political savy Determination	Generalist and appropriate specialist skills Social-personal, communications, and stylistic skills

*These skills are discussed at length in chapter 3. While these are the primary skills needed to perform well, there may be others as well.

Chapter Three
Basic Working Skills

Tis God gives skill
But not without men's hands;

He would not make
Antonio Stradivari's violins
without Antonio.

—Stradivarius

SKILLS EMPLOYERS ARE LOOKING FOR

Each worker, to be worth hiring and promoting, must have something to offer. This is your bank of skills. You are hired for your skills and potential, not because of your degree or experience, although both of these help establish your credentials or at least open the door to an interview. What's really impressive is what you can do and what other people say you can do. (The best jobs, and especially those requiring increasing responsibility, are very much in the hands of a few people who check you out with a few other people by telephone.) The more skills the better. The five categories of skills include job- and professional-related skills, social-personal skills, communication skills, work programming and management skills, and stylistic skills. Not everyone can or needs to possess all of them, however. But each person does need to assess his or her skills and decide which ones are missing, how and where to use those they have, and which new ones to master.

Table 3.1 shows the results of a survey taken by the Illinois chapter of the American Institute of Planners on the hiring practices of 144 employers of planners.

An important thing to remember is that employers have two basic objectives. They want competent employees. And they want loyal and "safe" employees. There is no room in government service for boat

Table 3.1. Most Often Cited Level of Influence for Each Criterion by Planning Position

Hiring criteria	Degree of influence at each level			
	Director	Senior	Middle	Entry
Undergraduate major	Moderate	Strong	Strong	Strong
Master's degree	Strong	Strong	Moderate	Slight
Doctorate	No	No	No	No
Graduate—AIP school	No	No	No	No
AIP member—full	No	No	No	No
AIP member—associate	No	No	No	No
School grades	No	Moderate	Moderate	Strong
References of friend	Slight	Slight	Slight	Slight
References in general	Strong	Strong	Strong	Strong
Appearance	Moderate	Moderate	Moderate	Moderate
School's reputation	Slight	Slight	Slight	Slight
Course of study	Moderate	Moderate	Strong	Strong
Writing ability	Strong	Strong	Strong	Strong
Speaking ability	Strong	Strong	Strong	Moderate
Experience	Strong	Strong	Strong	Slight
Outside activities	No	Slight	Slight	Slight
Publications	Slight	Slight	Slight	No
Graphics ability	Slight	Slight	Slight	Slight
Familiar with federal programs	Strong	Moderate	Slight	Slight

(How to read the table: The largest number of respondents indicated, for instance, that a familiarity with federal programs had a strong influence on their decision to hire a director or chief planner.)

Source: Leo Sterk and Carl V. Patton, "Hiring the Complete Planner," *Planning and Public Policy,* Vol. 5, No. 4, November 1979. Bureau of Urban and Regional Planning Research, University of Illinois at Urbana-Champaign.

rocking, radical chic, disagreeable behavior and chance taking. So, in addition to the following roster on marketable skills, you also need to think about your personal attributes, your sociopolitical, and your stylistic skills.

A word of advice, too, on the value of patience. If your boss is reluctant to give you the responsibility you think you should have, or won't let you go out into the community to talk to the public, it's probably because you haven't been on the job long enough to be fully "tested." Superiors want to be sure, without any doubt, that you come across as mature and competent. If your boss seems cautious, it is well to let a little time pass for him or her to be sure about your competence and style. For it is for style, as well as for your skills, you were hired in the first place.

Following are the five categories of skills you will want to study. Elsewhere in this book is a self-evaluation form that permits you to record your roster of skills and to identify those you might like to acquire (see Figure 6.5).

Job- and Profession-Related Skills

There are three subcategories of skills worth mastering. This is especially good advice if you aspire to be a top-level manager or administrator.

GENERALIST SKILLS. These skills include the background needed to know why you are doing what you are doing and for whom. To some extent, generalist skills are learned on the job. But the most effective generalists have academic or professional degrees, are liberally educated, and are familiar with the literature and central ideas associated with the work they are doing.

The crucial generalist skills include: *(a)* research skills, including literature searches, general surveys, and listening for and recording information; *(b)* identifying problems, issues, and goals; *(c)* considering alternative courses of action; *(d)* determining what needs to be done, why, and for whom; and *(e)* developing priorities.

SPECIALIST SKILLS. These are the skills needed to perform the tasks assigned and/or to match the job description of a particular position. Each government function requires its own specialists. While agency managers may not be specialists in anything, they cannot manage without a roster of trained persons who are experienced in the specialty areas. Examples of specialists are social workers in a public housing and community development agency; chemists in an air pollution control district; and highway engineers in a state transportation department. In each case, the specialist is especially trained to carry out a well-defined technical task or service. Their effectiveness depends primarily upon their prior professional training and education and only in part on their on-the-job experience.

NEW TECHNOLOGY SKILLS. Skills are needed to keep up with new methods or processes and to utilize new equipment. In our fast-moving and fast-changing society, new ways are constantly discovered to do things, new processes and methods to learn, and especially new equipment to utilize and master. Computer applications especially come to mind as does the environmental impact assessment process.

Social-Personal Skills

To work effectively among others no matter what the setting, one ought to be able to *(a)* cope effectively with stress, *(b)* cope with difficult people, *(c)* foster interpersonal relations, and *(d)* handle client services effectively and be responsive to client needs.

Communication Skills

On the job, you need to be generally aware of many skills and should be able to perform one or more of the following: *(a)* write memos and reports in jargon-free, clear English; *(b)* draft, draw, and communicate graphically and with film; *(c)* speak before the public; *(d)* facilitate dialogue in meetings; *(e)* give and follow directions; *(f)* run a meeting; and *(g)* work with the public.

Work Programming and Management Skills

If you are in a supervisorial or management post, you need to be able to understand and address the following: *(a)* work programming, coordination and scheduling, getting things done; *(b)* time management; *(c)* organizational planning and development (office management); and *(d)* job or project monitoring. You will also need to show skills in *(a)* effective leadership and supervision; *(b)* employee development and the orienting of new people to the job and the agency; *(c)* employee utilization and job satisfaction; *(d)* delegation of authority and responsibility; and *(e)* team building. Other areas of importance are *(a)* budgeting and fiscal management; *(b)* conflict resolution through negotiating, brokering, and mediating; *(c)* communicating with others; giving directions effectively; and *(d)* inspiring loyalty.

Stylistic Skills

At the heart of the question of effectiveness are the stylistic skills of attitude, aptitude, a positive approach to problem-solving and to work, good work habits, good judgment, the ability to command respect for your own participation and contributions, and the capacity to monitor and assess your own performance. No matter how skilled as a generalist, no matter how well trained as a manager or communications expert, you cannot expect to lend support to, assist, or influence others; effect change; mediate differences; sell new ideas; facilitate the support of decisionmakers; or please your client if you are surly, lazy, insensitive to the needs of others, arrogant or patronizing, a poor listener, or a neurotic and obsessive talker. Your style as an employee is crucial not only as it influences whether your job is done well but as it affects your own capacity to grow and develop professionally. In short, your personal style needs watching just as much as your writing and your research skills. If your style gets in the way of your personal objectives or those of your client, you may be faced with a decision about what to do to change.

ESSENTIAL SKILLS FOR SURVIVAL ON THE JOB

The most essential work skills of the job are communication skills, research skills, and work programming and management skills.

Communication Skills

First and foremost is the *word*. Whether in memos, reports, technical studies, oral presentations, the important thing is that whatever message is attempted, it must be understood. Voltaire said: ''We have a natural right to make use of our pens, as of our tongue, at our peril, risk and hazard.''

GIVING AND FOLLOWING DIRECTIONS. Since you may not be addressing the multitudes in your first few months on the job, the most

important communication skill you will need first is the ability to communicate with other individuals and especially co-workers. At this point of the game, you will probably need to use your ears twice as much as your mouth. Can you really take directions? Do you listen all the way through? Do you ask questions about any details you don't understand or do you just grab the gist of what is said to you? If you find that the people you work with and for are frequently misunderstanding you and vice versa, then you need to work harder to make sure understanding is taking place.

Check on whether you both understand the content of the directions before leaving the subject. For example, when your supervisor gives you a task, summarize his or her request in your own words. Sometimes you have to try an interpretation which goes beyond what was said, because many people make no allowance for the gap between their experience (standard operating procedure) and yours (what's going on here?).

A sample conversation might be:

Boss. I want you to review that report on Frobisher's Lousewart for me.

New Staff Person. I guess you want me to analyze it in memo form for you.

Boss. Yah, sure, that's the way we do it here.

New Staff Person. In that case, I suppose you want it for your section's report to the Advisory Board. How soon do you need it before the meeting?

Boss. People in my section always get their stuff to me at least four working days before a meeting.

New Staff Person. O.K., I think I'm clear on what you want, but to make sure is there anything else you think I ought to know about this task?

Boss. Oh yea, make sure that the typist circulates copies of your memo to all the other section chiefs.

Virtually everyone who is new on a job has been confronted with a similar situation where it would take a mind reader to do the task right, given the incompleteness of the original instructions.

COMMUNICATING UPWARD. Even more difficult is giving directions when you are trying to communicate something you know so well to a person who knows little or nothing about the subject. When you are speaking to a superior, such as a chief administrator or a politician, you often run into James' *Law of Ignorance* which states: ''The time taken for a clever man to influence a stupid man is inversely proportional to the gap in their knowledge.''[1] The key ingredient here is perserverance, patience, and tact. Valuable experience can be gained if you attended a large university with a hierarchy of deans. Even trying to get a small change in the status quo through channels can be a valuable training experience.[2]

Imagine, for example, trying to obtain permission to have a used sofa purchased and placed in the student lounge. You'll find that the matter will circulate through in-baskets rather slowly, and a great deal of attention and debate will ensue over insurance impacts, whether university policy requires bidding or purchase of the sofa from the state prison system, whether floor cleaning costs will mount significantly if a precedent like a sofa purchase is approved and so on. But ultimately a decision will filter down, because this is the kind of nitty-gritty detail deans and administrators can really sink their teeth into.

Then imagine trying to get credit for job experience as a substitute for a required course. When you suggest tampering with the curriculum, what will probably happen will be the formation of a study committee whose recommendations will be reviewed by subcommittees from the curriculum committee whose findings will be in turn surveyed by the school structure committee who will then probably report that a coordinating committee of faculty, students, and administrators should be formed to coordinate and study the different sets of committee reports. As a person who made the original suggestion, you'll inevitably be placed on several of the newly formed committees, which will give you tuition-free workshops useful in reducing your time spent influencing stupid people in the future.

WORKING WITH THE PUBLIC.   One situation rarely learned in schools is dealing with the public. Very often your first job will be one where you have to explain the rules of the game to someone who wants to do something that government regulates. For many ordinary citizens, this is their big face-to-face confrontation with government. You may make a lasting impression on some innocent taxpayer, which will add to the widely held feeling that government people are unresponsive and hard to deal with without an attorney to smooth the way.

Take, for example, the encounter between Flotilla Marsh, recently widowed homeowner, and Pincus Flornoy, the Variance, Exception and Special Permit Analyst II.

Flotilla. (huffing and puffing after a long search for the right bureau). Hello there, is this where I get a zoning variation?

Pincus. Well, that depends, what do you want to do?

Flotilla. I'm all alone since Hanibal, my husband died, and I'd like to convert my front bedroom and porch into a plant emporium and juice bar.

Pincus. Do you know your zoning?

Flotilla. What's that got to do with what I want to do?

Pincus. Well, we don't just hand out variances to anyone who asks. It depends on a lot of variables, including your existing zoning designation.

Flotilla. (visibly shaken). Well, could you look it up, please? I live at 314 Stone Street.

Pincus. Of course not, you'll need your assessor's parcel number and proof of ownership, such as a current tax bill. Then I can locate your place in our map books. The assessor is in our downtown annex; so you'd better hurry if you want to get there before they close.

Flotilla. I've already come clear across town on the bus to see you. Couldn't you help me while I'm here? Could you, for instance, call the assessor for me?

Pincus. I'm sorry, we don't offer that service in this section. We only process applications from bona fide property owners. Its your responsibility to establish that as a prerequisite to making application under the requisite sections of the zoning ordinance.

(Flotilla grips her shopping bag and leaves muttering imprecations about snotty bureaucrats.)

Technically, Pincus was playing by the rules. But in terms of human relations, his treatment of Flotilla Marsh was a disaster. Here are three of his mistakes.

1. *He was uncooperative* and gave poor directions. His job is to give people who come in all the available information. It would not have been out of line from the standpoint of decency to have checked out the zoning himself after phoning in for the parcel number, or to have let Mrs. Marsh use his phone to do it, rather than giving her a runaround. We have all been mishandled by people in government whose approach to the public has been to make things as difficult as possible. The right thing to do is to make things as simple as possible for the public, even if you're not the least bit responsible for the system you have to work with. Consider people you deal with as clients and the profits as the psychic rewards that you'll get from helping someone cope with the complexity you understand better than they do. Fewer people will hate government, in general, and what you do for them, in particular.

2. *He engaged in evasions and put-downs.* Just because people don't know about the rules and jargon of your job is no reason to treat them

without respect. Public employees must often be educators, so communication can ultimately take place. Pincus was willing to educate Flotilla about the rules and barriers she'd have to overcome to get started with him, but she couldn't learn anything about what she really wanted to do without being brushed off. Many new employees consider this sort of thing an "objective attitude," when actually it's the essence of stonewalling unresponsiveness.

3. *He maintained his social distance* by speaking stilted jargon, instead of plain English. If one weren't put off by his uncooperative attitude, certainly resentment would build after having jargon, such as variables, existing zoning designation, bona fide, and requisite, thrown at you. If you think it's smart to pepper your conversation with the public with such two-bit words and phrases, you'll probably register just like the smart aleck in the fifth grade, whom everyone wanted to beat up at recess.

PRESENTING YOURSELF IN PUBLIC. Very often staff members have to venture out in public and communicate what their work is all about to people they want to persuade, inform, and positively impress. Very often they will antagonize, confuse, and negatively impress their audience. The seven deadly sins of presentation include the following:

1. The topic is confusing and unclear, often because it's been dragged out of a fat, unreadable report which hasn't been properly summarized or focused.
2. The presentation is so full of technical triple-ply language that only Ph.D.'s in the field can follow it.
3. Unreal topics and unasked questions are addressed. For example, a regional agency often traveled around to local meetings with a 30-minute slide show showing abstract maps which posed the question, "What Regional Form Do We Prefer?"
4. A tech fix is the kind of presentation where a lot of number crunching has gone on. There is all too often a temptation to insinuate a level of precision that isn't really there. This is often the case when projections and mathematical modeling results are presented to lay people by the technicians who are stakeholders in the number-crunching business.[3]
5. Solutions are often offered that hide important considerations. For example, a capital improvement program might be presented as easily affordable. The unseen assumption is that inflation is nonexistant in future building costs.
6. Very often a recommendation for the future will be presented by dismissing the current realities. For example, a neighborhood renewal

scheme for a low income neighborhood will be offered up as if its imple-mentation would mean residents would not have to give up many of their existing homes to get from here to there. Means are dismissed by ends.

7. A problem is minutely described, checked over, and defined, but the presentation lets things hang right there. No point of view on what needs to be done to alleviate this problem is given.

There are a few things to keep in mind when making a presentation:

1. Know what your subject is all about and what you are doing with it.

2. Know what you want to get from your presentation. Identify your audience and what the optimum response would be.

   Do you simply want to impart information?

   Do you want to offer advice?

   Do you want to get approval of some proposal?

3. Does your presentation allow openings for discussion and feedback from listeners? Are you prepared to handle it? Leave more time for discussion than presentation.

4. Is this timing of your presentation correct? Is it coming at the proper stage of the decision process? For example, would you make a pre-sentation showing the need for more funding for transit for the elderly a short time after the city council had finally adopted next year's budget—and still hope for prompt results?

5. Identify the highlights and focus on them in your presentation.

6. Don't distribute printed materials just before you're going to speak. Many of your audience will be reading when they should be listening.

7. Learn how to really listen to what people are saying in terms of their hidden feelings, as well as the surface verbal content. For example, people resisting assisted housing in their neighborhood may be talking about how damaging to property values cheaper assisted housing will be, when they really mean that they're afraid of having people who take welfare in this form as neighbors.

8. Don't be defensive or evasive when hard questions are asked. Even President Carter can say, "I don't know, but if you want me to, I'll find out."

WRITTEN COMMUNICATIONS. As public confidence in govern-ment has dropped, many critics have pointed out that government officials are often their own worst enemies when they try to communicate in writing. Anyone worth keeping on staff past probation should be able to write short memos, directives, and letters; brief, clear reports of medium length; and well-organized long reports.

The biggest problem is that all too many people who have to communicate ideas in writing can't do it clearly. Several types of deficiences are especially common in the use of English:

Jargon and Psuedo Scientific Prattle. In academic settings, one is rewarded for obscure, murky shop talk. After all, the authorities, whose texts you have to buy, write like that. For example:

> Thus, we conclude, as we began, that both of the two common and superficially different modes of defining a region express useful, if not indispensable, truths. The less metaphorical mode is content to delimit a region as that contiguous one having the necessary geographic unities; the people with sufficiently homogeneous desires, attitudes, and wants; the sufficient bases in natural and man-made resources and technology; and the appropriate voluntary institutions and governmental organization to achieve, within the limits and opportunities of the structure of external political power, the utmost efficiency in the fullest attainment of the major human values of the people of the area. To this comprehensive summation the rival or organismic mode of expression, drawing on the analogy of individual living organisms, adds an emphatic insistence that such an equilibrium of optimum efficiency in the satisfaction of human wants is not to be achieved unless people, values, institutions, and resources are structured into functional components, as interrelated and indespensable to each other and to the healthy functioning of the whole, and as pulse-like in the regularity of their interaction, as are the component parts of man and the animals.[4]

If prose such as this were put in a document for public discussion, the only response to be expected would be "What did he say?" or maybe just "What?" Yet, report after report is filled with the kind of pompous complexity that turns readers off.

That the prattle of academia reaches out into public writing is exemplified in this unpublished gem from an overpaid economic consultant in the San Francisco area, who wanted to sound like an irrefutable expert at any cost:

> The appropriate concepts of cost and gain depend on the level of optimization and the alternative policies that are admissable. The appropriate level of optimization and the alternatives that should be compared depends on a general acceptance of suitable criterion.

While the sentence length is not up to academic standards, the denseness of language was at the Ph.D. level. Here's how it might be rewritten in clearer language:

> The notion of an optimum cost-benefit ratio really depends on how one defines a benefit. The level of benefits from each of various alternatives depends on the standards accepted for use as a comparison.

Legalese or Complexosis. Language can be so stilted, stuffy, and complex that it fogs instead of clarifies ideas or instructions. A good example of this is Section 6416 of the state of California's Housing Element Guidelines, presumably written for the guidance of local government people:

> In accordance with the provisions of Article 4, a housing program consisting of a comprehensive problem solving strategy adopted by the local governing body which both establishes local housing goals, policies and priorities aimed at alleviating unmet needs and remedying the housing problem, and sets forth the course of action which the locality is undertaking and intends to undertake to effectuate these goals, policies and priorities. Making adequate provision for the housing needs of all economic segments in the community to plan affirmatively, through its housing element program for a balanced housing supply suited to the needs of the community as defined in Section 6418 of these regulations.[5]

There are three basic faults with language infected with complexosis. First, the sentences contain more than one thought each. Second, there are cross references to things like Article 4 and Section 6418 which murk up the meaning of this section. Finally, there are newly minted word combinations strung together to produce important sounding meaninglessness, for example, a comprehensive problem solving strategy. How does a locality meet this requirement? Many government documents are written in a sort of legalese—the language of law, which retired Yale University professor Fred Rodell described as "almost deliberately designed to confuse and muddle the ideas it purports to convey." In a 1939 book titled *Woe Unto You, Lawyers!* he wrote:

> No segment of the English Language in use today is so muddy, so confusing, so hard to pin down to its supposed meaning as the language of the law. It ranges only from the ambiguous to the completely uncomprehensible. . . .Yet why should people not be privileged to understand completely and precisely any written laws that directly concern them, any business documents they have to sign, any code of rules and restrictions which apply them and which they perpetually live?[6]

Bureaucratic Flapdoodle. A 12th-century French bishop wrote to his priests: "Be neither ornate nor flowery in your speech. . .or the educated will think you a boor and you will fail to impress the peasants."

The general idea is to try to write like you speak and therefore avoid pomposity. John O'Hayre reports that President Franklin D. Roosevelt was really rankled by bureaucratic flapdoodle, which he defined as oily talk, having a false look of genuineness. He once got the following memo on what federal workers were supposed to do in case of an air raid:

> Such preparations as shall be made as will completely obscure all Federal buildings and non-Federal buildings occupied by the Federal government during an air raid for any period of time from visability by reason of internal or external illumination. Such obscuration may be obtained either by blackout construction or by termination of the illumination.

FDR simplified this monstrosity as follows:

> Tell them that in buildings where they have to keep the work going to put something over the windows; and in buildings where they can let the work stop for a while, turn out the lights.[7]

Not only memos are afflicted with filigree language. Annual reports often sound as pompous as the funeral oration for a Roman emperor. Here's one from a New England town planning department:

> This agency's activities during the preceding year were primarily oriented to continuing their primary functions of informing local groups and individuals to acquaint them of their needs, problems, and alternate problem solutions, in order that they can effect decisions in planning and implementing a total program that will best meet the needs of the people now and in the future.

An uncurling of this peace of pomposity might read:

> We spent most of our time last year working with local people, going over their problems and trying to help them figure out solutions. In this way, we hoped to help them set up and carry out a program that will solve today's problems and also satisfy tomorrow's needs.

Buzz Words and Abstract Writing. It's important to use concrete words with specific meanings. Buzz words are words that may have many meanings but mean nothing specific. They can make a communication just blunder about without any real meaning. Party platforms, patriotic speeches, and real estate sales brochures are common examples of this kind of mindless burbling. However, technocrats often use this technique to fuzz up whatever original meaning there might have been in an attempt to inform the laity. For example, an environmental impact report tried to explain economic impacts as follows:

> The economic effects, although extremely important, are often so subtle and so confounded with other environmental effects, we neither realize nor appreciate the true economic effects and the resulting advantages of properly recognizing their linkage with environmental conditions.

The problem here is that the word *effects* has become a pure abstraction having been used three different ways in a single sentence. Some

Figure 3.1. 100 Tired Terms

1. Centroid
2. Feedback
3. Ecological
4. Morphological
5. Activity mode
6. Intrinsic
7. Image
8. Disjointed
9. Linkage
10. Polarity
11. Trade off
12. Linear
13. Input-output
14. Dichotomy
15. Subcenter
16. Continuum
17. Action program
18. Economic base
19. Mobility
20. Urban structure
21. Systemic
22. Synthesis
23. Normative
24. Hierarchical
25. Tertiary
26. Habitat
27. Environs
28. Expertise
29. Maximization
30. Optimization
31. Comprehensibility
32. Conurbation
33. CBD (Central business district)
34. Urban pattern
35. Revitalize
36. Growth poles
37. Trade-offs
38. Systems approach
39. Econometrics
40. Development theory
41. Protypical
42. Movement system
43. Social overhead
44. Distributive system
45. Cityscape
46. Urban character
47. Human scale
48. Master planned
49. Planned community
50. Level of effort
51. Urban path
52. Landmark
53. Human needs
54. Value system
55. Small town character
56. Inequability
57. Interface
58. Restructuring
59. Nondirective
60. Individualized
61. Resource-intensive
62. Sector
63. Multi-disciplinary
64. Self-contained
65. Conceptualized
66. Disadvantaged
67. Orchestrated
68. Evidential
69. Empirical or Stochastic
70. Manpower
71. Framework
72. Determinism
73. Incrementalized
74. Finalized
75. Procurement
76. Interpretative
77. Sensitivity-analysis
78. Dialogue
79. Citizen inputs
80. Guidelines
81. Infrastructure
82. Thrust
83. Reoriented
84. Certification
85. Prescribed
86. Rationale
87. Harmonized
88. Substantive
89. Viable
90. Documentation
91. Spectrum
92. Budgetary
93. Parameters
94. Prioritize
95. Agendized
96. Evaluative process
97. Imageability
98. Multimodal
99. Publicly determined
100. Limited success

words are so commonly and badly used in certain fields that they often become part of a semantic charade. Figure 3.1 contains a list of words urbanists and other technocrats have given so many meanings that they've lost most of their clarity. They need to be retired for a while until they regain some meaning.

Overcoming Illiteracy. Given the growing deterioration of basic writing skills among college students, it's not surprising that much of what is written in government agencies is not only sloppy, but virtually illiterate. One county department head used to set aside one day per week to rewrite the staff reports of subordinates. He complained that many of his staff, who were college graduates, expected the secretaries, who were high school graduates, to "fix up their mistakes" in grammar, spelling, punctuation, and in many cases be their personal editors! Sometimes semi-illiterates rise to the top, and there's no one over them to set things right. Here's an example from a county planning director's paper on rural development and how it might have been rewritten by someone with basic English skills (unfortunately, he wrote just as he spoke).

> At the outset of any discussion relative to concluding peripheral city or town land use, one must acknowledge the controversy that is generally generated by such a discussion, especially when City (all cities) and County legislators are involved. The tangents, all mind boggling are numerous and relate to many frames of reference of the past, present and future wherein quite frequently during any forum the context of any statement may be read a half dozen ways. In generating a functional formula that has some flexible application around the County for *total* County *application* (a very important thought) County Staff must deal with the following thoughts, acts, or proposals:

> (Biggest thought) There are diverse attitudes in all eight cities. In the past (and somewhat in the present) all cities that are experiencing growth have annexed following older development plans for the sole purpose of accommodating development. There has been little concern as to affects on contiguous unincorporated lands, such as speculations, taxation, incompatibility with agriculture, etc. Overnight with new state laws (LAFCo mandates) the County is called upon to reverse past trends on a wholesale basis. In most instances the cities in a plural form say, "we must bite the bullet and resolve the question of peripheral city land use, when really that we is you the county. All cities and the county should solicit the State to pass legislation enabling cities to annex everything within their sphere of influence and zone it for greenbelt with a corresponding order to the assessor to reduce taxation.

And as it might have been rewritten:

> Land use on the city borders is controversial, especially when city councilmembers and county supervisors are involved. In attempting to devise a solution that would be applicable everywhere in the county, county staff must contend with the following conditions:

> a. The cities do not all think the same about this subject.
> b. Cities that are expanding have annexed and accommodated development with little provision for the effects on the surrounding unincorporated areas.
> c. Now new state laws, such as the Local Agency Formation Commission Act mandates, require the county to reverse these effects. However, in most instances, the cities want the county to solve the problem of controlling development at the fringe by itself, until they can annex

such lands. Therefore, all jurisdictions should try to get state legislation passed enabling cities to annex all lands within their spheres of influence, hold it as greenbelt, and corespondingly order the assessor to reduce the assessments on such lands.

Research Skills for Public Policy

Anyone working at a professional or technical level must have the ability to generalize from available data and observation and at the outset know what data is needed and what is not. You should fully understand the nature of the problem you're trying to analyze and solve and have the ability to attack it in an intellectually creative fashion. The following ideas on how to do this would probably not be observed or taught at most universities.

PLAN YOUR RESEARCH.   Research at work does not consist of just compiling a lot of ready-made facts, with analysis coming at a later and separate stage. Facts do not mean anything until their meaning and significance for a definite purpose are understood. They only acquire meaning as part of the answer to specific questions. Unless one has clearly framed these questions before one starts to compile data, the data will probably be a lot of useless information. For example, in one newly incorporated city, the planning commission decided that they could do a general plan with citizen volunteers. So they set about to count everything in the city: fire plugs, telephone booths, and miles of pavement. When they had completed the inventory taking, they called in a consultant and said: "We've got all the data, how many days will it take for you to work it up into a plan for the city that meets state requirements?" "The same amount of time as if you hadn't done it because most of this data is useless for what a plan would address. You've gone in for a blind collection of facts without even a classification system. For example, you have all the miles of roads in the city measured, but you haven't classified or mapped them by number of lanes, whether they are local, gas tax eligible, or state highways, or whether they're even public or private. I'd have to start all over again, if I were to work here," he replied.

DON'T SET ARTIFICIAL LIMITS ON SCOPE.   When studying a jurisdiction with boundaries, it's important to avoid the trap of erecting airtight limits at the boundaries. You must remain conscious of the relationship of the jurisdiction to other areas and policies outside the borders.

One West Coast city, for example, had its blinders on so tight that its plan called for high-density residential development on its half of an island, under the approach zone of the adjoining international airport's runways. The plan made no mention of the island's having an airport, and when the city approved the type of development shown on the plan, the airport sued. The judge declared the plan a nullity after noting that it made the city more of an island than it really was.

RESEARCH SHOULD AFFECT HUMAN ACTIVITY.   Research should be aimed at human affairs and activities, and the results should be expressed as such rather than abstractions such as visitor days, trip ends, marginal costs, rock formations, and density ranges.

RESEARCH SHOULD BE FUTURE ORIENTED.   The research is only valuable in so far as it sheds light on what should be done in the future. (The future starts with the moment after this one.) Too much research has been an exquisite investigation and extrapolation of the past and does not shed much light on where do we go from here.

FACTS NEED TO HAVE A BACKGROUND.   It's useless to know the average income per capita in an area without knowing whether it's rising, falling, evenly distributed, or skewed, and how it compares with other places.

THERE IS NO SUCH THING AS PURE ANALYSIS.   For many technicians, there is a tendency to feel that evidence which cannot be expressed as numbers resulting from rigorous methodology is of small

value. They tend to overemphasize quantitative answers in situations where quantitative judgments are essential. The researcher must be able to deal with questions of "why?" as well as "what?" and "how much?" Too much use of methodology unaccompanied by clear explanation usually has the effect of rendering the work useless to policymakers. C. Northcote Parkinson describes this technique of delay as follows:

> The techniques of delay have been strengthened in the modern world by the current emphasis on research. In matters scientific, the first rule, as we know, is to discover the facts. The same rule, as applied to human problems, means that a crime wave is not a matter of principle but of measurement. If Negroes riot in Los Angeles our first reaction is to count the Negroes, our second to decide whether they are as black as they are painted. That fact-finding is thus a substitute for decision is very generally known. What we fail to recognise is that fact-finding is also a substitute for thought.[8]

PUTTING YOURSELF IN CHARGE

Before you advance to any real management responsibilities, you should know whether you can make yourself into an effective and efficient section of one. There are some basic skills which you should master. The first is being able to do a fixed amount of work in a fixed amount of time and for a specific amount of money. To be effective, you must be doing the right things with your time. If you can do them without waste and on time, you're economic.

Be realistic, and don't bite off more than you can chew. Break up the big jobs with little chores that you can do in 15 minutes or less, so you'll feel you're producing something every day. Know what kind of work you like to do and the kind you would put off if you could. Be sure the desirable and easy work doesn't eat up the time for the less desirable chores. This requires the kind of discipline few of us applied in school (or even heard about before).

Time Management or Getting Organized

Many people will have all the skills mentioned earlier and still not be able to perform effectively on the job. Such persons are usually so busy being overwhelmed by the tasks at hand, that a request to take on a new assignment sends them into a catatonic state. Their work is characterized by two basic deficiencies. Either they don't get it done on time or they don't turn in finished work. If both deficiencies are present, this person is usually entering the terminal phase of his or her sojourn with any employer.

Effective use of your time is necessary to be productive and to meet deadlines. Time is one of the basic things you sell to any employer, and *you* need to take the primary responsibility for seeing that value is received for what you sell. This means *putting yourself in charge of yourself.* Only you can make yourself effective. In terms of time management, it means selecting the best task to do from all the possibilities available and then doing it straight away.

If making such a choice is difficult, make a list each day (or week) of the tasks you have to do (see Table 3.2). Assign priorities to each one, such as 1, 2, or 3 (you can also use A, B, C and so on). Break down the big tasks into steps that move toward completion. Stop and determine when your prime time for work occurs. Are you full of energy at 8 a.m., slack off in the p.m., or are you a slow starter who peaks about one hour after lunch? Once you know your bio-rhythm for work, do your top priority work in the prime time. This is not only the time when you're most alert, but when you should have the least interruptions. Most phone calls and people desiring to see you can wait, and many should.

Don't worry about completing your list. Accomplish all the 1s that you can. Be realistic about your working conditions and allow for interruptions and distractions. If there are too many, have a conference with your boss about getting some insulation from these work stoppers. It may mean moving your desk, getting permission to work at the public library or in the conference room, or even a flextime arrangement where you do some work outside the standard 8 to 5 shift.

Do the 2s and 3s in nonprime time. Some people bring such things along to do at boring meetings, while on hold on the telephone, or when they are on low energy such as after a big lunch. Don't use your prime time for churning out trivia, reading the newspaper, or answering inconsequential phone calls.

Try selecting at least one item from your number 3 priority list for oblivion each day or at least once per week. For example, you could skip doing a personnel evaluation for an employee who's left the state, going to a farewell coffee, filling out inane questionnaires from students who want you to do their research for them, and so on.

Table 3.2. A Sample Task Chart for a Blue Monday

Type of Task	Time	Code*	Examples of tasks
Call	8:00-9:00 A.M.	A (Important to Councilman Jones)	Citizens complaining about dog droppings on jogging trails
Follow up	8-9:30 A.M.	A – D	Memo to office of Councilman Jones re: calls and action taken on dog control on jogging trails.
Read and Review	9:30-10:00 A.M.	B – D	Read and comment on proposed new leash ordinance
Finish	10:30-12:00 A.M.	A – D	Report on bike trail standards in new subdivisions.
Lunch	12:00-1:00 A.M.	A – P	Happily because all D tasks were finished in A.M.—prime time.
Write	1:00-2:00 P.M.	B – P	Letters to other jurisdictions' planners re: bike trail planning
Read and Review	2:00-3:00 P.M.	C – P	Professional articles on bicycling as an alternative to autos. Prepare summary for Friday staff meeting.
Do	3:00-5:00 P.M.	B – P	Attend regional meeting for trail and path planners.

*A = highest priority, B = medium, C = lowest, P = preferred work, D = disliked.

NOTE: Prime time for handling difficult people or doing scut work is A.M. for this person. P.M.'s are when his biorhythms are down and he handles lighter chores. Peter Drucker warned, however, "Most of your time is not your own. Most work plans fail because we think we have all of the workday. Most of this time is [theirs.]" (From "Using time efficiently takes planning," *Indianapolis Star,* April 30, 1978.) Therefore, allow for interruptions by the public, co-workers, fire drills, and other distractions. Try, however, to get important high priority work done when such schedule impediments are least frequent. On really important work have the receptionist take callback messages or work some place sheltered such as a nearby library, or vacant office without a phone. (Undoubtedly the public's access to you by phone is a sacred right. But you have a sacred right to "not be in" for that two-hour period when you need to be productive and your biorhythms are right.)

Finally, you must begin to say no to procrastination by cleaning up your twos and threes first—daydreaming, reading, socializing, allowing constant interrupters to interrupt or, worst or all, saving the top priority tasks for a heroic last minute surge of effort in the same fashion you used to churn out term papers. Remember that in the real world *crash programs crash.* You and you alone can control your priorities.

Another hangover many people bring from school is the inability to do finished work. Inexperienced people may do important work just well enough to earn a passing grade by old school standards, but in most jobs, the system will grade your work on a pass or fail basis. Finished work means that it has no gaps, no details to be worked out by others later, no big "ifs" to perplex the user of the work. Finally, it should not be sent in in half-baked form, but should be coherent and hang together so that the client for the work (boss, elected officials, citizens) can sign, approve, or adopt the work without long explanations from you. Don't get in the habit of "getting sent back to the drafting board" for work that won't work. Don't bury your clients in voluminous reports, unprepared oral presentations, and innumerable unevaluated options. Use this simple test to test your work. If you were the boss, would you be willing to let this work go out with your name and professional reputation riding on it. If you have reasonable doubts, take it back and polish it a little more.

Remember, too, that progress reports (oral or with short notes or memos) as you go along allow conceptual matters to be addressed and issues resolved early in the process. When you're down to the wire on a deadline is not the time for you or anyone else to discover you still don't know who the client is, or what the main thrust of your work is, or to discover you and your boss are at fundamental odds about your approach to a job. Bosses don't like surprises so keep them informed regularly.

NOTES

1. Dennis James, *Bluff Your Way in Management* (London: Wolfe Publishing Ltd., 1969), pp. 17-18.

2. Alfred Kahn said, "Deans are to a faculty as hydrants are to dogs." (From a news story in the Portland *Oregonian,* February 28, 1978.) However, to an imaginative student, deans can be a great teaching resource for a later career in a large hierarchical organization.

3. Very often such technocrats will continue to offer tentative decisions that are always precise, but wrong. More variables must be considered on the next run of the model.

4. The Directive Committee on Regional Planning, *The Case for Regional Planning* (New Haven: Yale University Press, 1947), pp. 35-36.

5. California Department of Housing and Community Development, *Housing Element Manual* (Sacramento: March 1978), p. 53.

6. Stuart Auerbach, "War on Legalese Gaining Adherents," *Los Angeles Times,* January 29, 1978, p. 2.

7. John O'Hayre, *Gobbledygook Has Got to Go* (Washington, D.C.: U.S. Government Printing Office, 1966), p. 39.

8. C. Northcote Parkinson, *The Law of Delay: Interviews and Outerviews* (New York: Houghton Mifflin Co., 1970), pp. 121-122. Copyright 1970 by C. Northcote Parkinson.

Chapter Four
Essential Management
Skills

*"Government after all is a simple
thing"—Warren G. Harding, quoted by
Justice Felix Frankfurter who added,
"There never was a more pathetic mis-
apprehension of responsibility than
Harding's touching statement."*

Some politicians waft in and out of government with no more idea of what's involved than Warren G. Harding, but increasingly the person on the payroll is going to have to understand his or her responsibilities more fully than ever before. This chapter will outline some of the essential skills that you'll have to master in order to be a manager. The term manager refers to "one who conducts business affairs with economy and care."

Programming and Budgeting in General

In today's world, economy is mentioned in more places than the diction-ary. The first skill required is being able to assess whether or not to have a program at all (program feasibility).

Here are the basic steps. (We'll use a housing rehabilitation program as an example.)

WHAT IS IT YOU'RE TRYING TO DO?   This question should be broken down into its component parts. How much of anything will the program cover? If you're setting up a housing rehabilitation loan pro-gram, for example, how many homeowners will be reached by the available funds? What is it going to do? Be sure of the scope, impact, and the availability of resources to run a program. How many dilapidated

houses are there in need of repair? Are neighborhood conditions such
that owners would be willing to invest in rehabilitation? Even if they did,
how much would it take to change the downward slide of any particular
neighborhood. Are there side effects, like rent increases for low income
people who couldn't afford them? Know precisely what you are trying to
do before letting the program see daylight.

FOR WHOM? Who would be the clients? Owner-occupied or
renter-occupied housing? Medium- or low-income families? Where?
What is involved politically and socially?

FOR HOW MUCH? Who will do the work? How many loans
could you handle with present budget and staff? Could you get more? If
so what would it do to the administrative cost for each rehabilitation
project? How much would be repaid by loan payments? Federal grant
money? How much would be local "hard" money?

**UNDER WHAT CONDITIONS WOULD A FEASIBLE PRO-
GRAM WORK?** Do you need cooperation from other jurisdictions,
departments, agencies, and/or the federal government? Is the necessity for
getting continual clearances and authorizations, plus the constant paperwork going to be a formidable barrier to fixing up anyone's home? Can
your agency find enough reputable contractors who will take on little
jobs? Can the agency handle disputes, inspections, faulty work, and
other problems likely to arise between owners and contractors?

WHY? Can you spell out clearly what ends the program is aimed at
achieving and the likelihood of their success? Can you convince a hard-
nosed budget analyst that the money will be better spent in this program
than in others competing for the same local funds or federal grants?

Developing a Work Program

Let's assume that your project has been given approval to proceed in
principle. The next thing you'll be required to do is a work program that
will work. A checklist for developing one includes the following:

WHAT IS THE FINAL PRODUCT GOING TO BE? A report? If
so, what will it contain? Proposals, research findings, executive summary
or abstract (always include this), maps, graphs, tables, and so on? Is the

documentation and source material going to be published in the report or as a separate technical report?

How will you tell your story when the product is finished. This is the time to think of what graphics, filmstrips, maps, and other public presentation materials you'll want to illustrate your main points.

What will your distribution scheme be for the public, policymakers and other technicians.

It's a good idea to avoid fat reports; they generally get ignored by the people who are supposed to read them. How will the report be released to the media? It's important to know how to write a good press release, since most reporters would rather report on a conflict than on the contents of any program, if left to their own devices.

If the budget allows, an inexpensive tabloid edition for the public with a mail-back form for reaction is usually satisfactory. The policymakers and other important people get the full, typeset version with executive summary, while other technicians, organizations, archives, and libraries should receive a mimeographed or xeroxed technical supplement which shows all the techniques, statistics, data sources, and other documentation which validate the recommendations of the policymaker's report.

Discussion drafts are a very good idea politically, as well as technically, because it allows corrections and important revisions from participants in the review process to be incorporated. Since many of the changes will be semantic, it's important for the writers to swallow pride of authorship when faced with these nit-picking editorial changes. It is more important to maintain support for the program recommendations. Drafts for discussion only are also good as trial balloons, to get debate going and discover the nature of the opposition, while fallback positions are still possible. Program recommendations which surface later have a lesser chance of surviving the political process because the talking and negotiating stage of dealing with critics and opponents is bypassed and you're playing a zero sum game—namely, that some interest must lose in order for the other to win. This is a situation political people abhor, and the likelihood of having all the work that went into the program pigeonholed is increased substantially by ignoring the need for dealing with possible controversy at the onset.

WHAT ARE YOU GOING TO WORK WITH?

Availability of Existing Data. What is its quality? Is it current or obsolete? Once you know this, you can set the level of precision at which you're going to have to work. If new data is going to be needed, be sure you know how much it's going to cost and decide whether it's worth the cost. If there's still uncertainty (and there usually is), then determine how much pursuit of data you're going to allow. Some data compilation addicts undergo a researcher's version of "rapture of the deep" when allowed to immerse themselves in a sea of statistics without restraints on when they have to surface and be reviewed for significant results.

People.   Who is going to do the work? People in your department, other agencies' staff, consultants, temporary unexperienced or fulltime experienced people? Know who's going to be able to do what, when. In many bureaucratic organizations, new work has a hard time fitting in, because the standard operating procedures (SOPs) insure that regular work will expand to fill the time available. How is the work going to be coordinated if it has to flow between people in different departments, consultants, citizen advisory groups, and budget reviewers to get done? Very often you will have the responsibility for getting work out from various sovereign entities, when your authority doesn't extend beyond the power to plead. Be sure your authority to get the job done matches your responsibility. If authority must be shared, then so should responsibility. One good way to be sure that blame for delays is properly placed is to devise a work flowchart, that all can agree upon. Figure 4.1 shows a chart used for producing reports, that stopped a lot of bickering and blame games in one agency.

Time.   How fast is the product or any part of it really needed?[1] Is the decision chain of finding answers really a continuous revision of preconceptions? Allow time for education and missionary work to overcome this situation. Are there important external events that may change the fate of the program? (For example, an election that may remove supporters from office or a grant for a three-year project only funded on a year-to-year basis.) Sometimes it may be well to stretch projects out so that they can reach logical cutoff points before completion. Do not use too large a budget in any one year if it will make the project a political target. Stretching out the work also may let the program results emerge after enemies are out of office. (This is called the ploy of letting the dinosaurs die off.)[2] In determining the time needed for each piece of work, such devices as PERT (Program Evaluation and Review Technique) and critical path charts are useful, if they're not permitted to get too complex.

A simple critical path for part of the report production process

Figure 4.1. Production of Reports Procedure

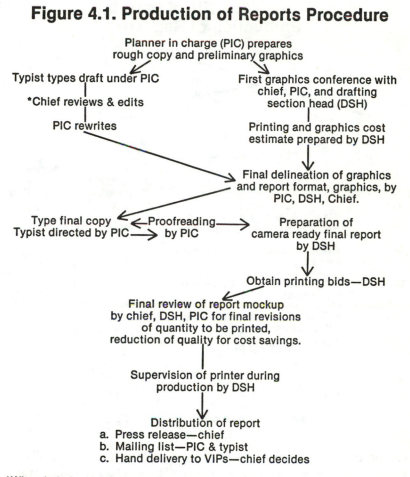

Planner in charge (PIC) prepares
rough copy and preliminary graphics

Typist types draft under PIC

*Chief reviews & edits

PIC rewrites

First graphics conference with
chief, PIC, and drafting
section head (DSH)

Printing and graphics cost
estimate prepared by DSH

Final delineation of graphics
and report format, graphics, by
PIC, DSH, Chief.

Type final copy ←Proofreading→
Typist directed by PIC→ by PIC

Preparation of
camera ready final report
by DSH

Obtain printing bids—DSH

Final review of report mockup
by chief, DSH, PIC for final revisions
of quantity to be printed,
reduction of quality for cost savings.

Supervision of printer during
production by DSH

Distribution of report
a. Press release—chief
b. Mailing list—PIC & typist
c. Hand delivery to VIPs—chief decides

*When he's involved, the section chief makes final decisions. All others are
delegated to PIC or DSH as indicated.

described in the Production of Reports procedure (Figure 4.1) can be seen
in Figure 4.2. The critical path here requires 12 working days and
follows the sequence of activities A-D-G, which means that the planner in
charge (PIC) has the critical schedule.

Project Direction. Management is depending on others to produce
work you're responsible for sending out as finished. If working with
others this way is not suitable to your personality, avoid promotions to
management jobs. When you are the one in charge of seeing the work
gets done, then ''seeing'' becomes part of your job. Periodically (every-

Figure 4.2. Critical Path to Production of Reports

Job	Job Description	Immediately Preceeding Job	Normal Time (In Working Days)
A₃	Planner in charge does rough copy. Two preliminary graphics	Start	3
B₆	Graphics, prepares maps, report format	Start	6
C₂	First graphics conference and cost estimate	Start	2
D₅	PIC and chief edit and rewrite, PIC does final copy	A	5
E₂	DSH makes Final Report, obtains bids	C	2
F₇	Distribution list by chief and PIC	A	7
G₄	Print and distribute report	BDE	4

day or every week depending on tightness of schedule) see the other people on the project and their work. Ask at least three questions: ''What exactly have you been doing since I last talked to you?''''Why?''''When are you going to finish?'' Some people thrust into supervisory positions are reluctant to ask these questions or to ''bird dog'' a task. They either don't last long or they shouldn't.

The first question established whether or not you and the other person have the same understanding of what's supposed to be produced. Often, directions that you thought were perfectly clear were misunderstood, and it's vital to get things back on track before too much detouring has occurred. Some people can't stay on track very long before they go spinning off on a tangent. This is particularly true of bright, creative, and ''artistic'' people (often generalists with no responsible experience but with lots of ideas and good intentions) who like to improvise, rather than "cook by the book." It's important to make sure that all team members understand how and why their pieces fit into the bigger picture. Always listen, obtain feedback, and be open to fresh ideas from people who are doing the work. Don't be a know-it-all who only issues commands. Be a coordinator rather than a supervisor. Sometimes this means you work for someone who is under you on the organization chart to remove obstacles, resolve delays and priority conflicts, and get things done!

When you ask someone why they're doing the work, you are checking on whether there's still a common understanding of the objectives for doing the work. Define these objectives in terms of what specific things you want to have finished at specific times in the course of the project.

When you ask when are you going to finish, it's important to remember that there's a fine line between nagging and taking a continuing interest in one's work. Remember people rarely have only your project to work on and even more rarely do they have complete control over their time. If someone is getting bogged down because they're getting conflicting demands, get it settled immediately with the person caught in the cross fire. Only the individuals doing the work have the ability to know what their work pace is and what their obligations to other jobs are. You need to negotiate for completion dates and *get a commitment* for such deadlines. Not only will people working in government have to meet standards of productivity, but they will have to take on the additional responsibility for getting their work done accurately, on time, and in finished form. Completed staff work means presenting answers, not questions, to the person who reviews the work. The junior person should take the responsibility for writing so that the senior person will be able to concentrate on the content rather than being diverted by the need to correct spelling, grammar, sentence structure, and composition. Completed staff work is something a senior person could feel confident in signing, rather than editing and reworking. Rough drafts are not precluded, but they should not be half-baked excuses for shifting the work up to the senior level. It's essential to know what you're going to do as project manager. Allow a certain amount of time for putting out fires and running interference that other members of the team cannot handle, but set priorities for your own production, too. You must see that your time is as correctly budgeted as anyone else's on the project team.

You will need to learn to review other people's work. Do so orally first, then read what they've written. Would you feel comfortable staking your professional reputation on the reception this work would receive when it leaves the office? If not, ask tough questions of the authors until you're satisfied the inconsistencies and errors in the work have been combed out, and the work is ready for review and criticism on questions of policy, rather than quality. Make sure the team gets to review your work in the same strong light.

Meetings

Staff meetings in government are all too often either one way reporting, ego monologues, or boring round robin show-and-tell exercises where everyone's critical faculties are checked at the door by group consensus.

There are only two reasons for taking time to have a staff meeting:

1. To make sure everyone gets the same information simultaneously and that everyone understands the message.
2. To put ideas and finished work up for review by the whole project team or department. This should test the work as a whole before informed but critical colleagues and show up any major flows. It also bestows recognition on people who've done important work, but who won't share the public limelight.

It's important to have a group that is more diverse than like-minded peers, because peers may all share the same blindspot. For example, the staff of a major city planning department reviewed the expensive materials on the comprehensive plan that were to be sent out to each district in the city for citizen workshops. None of them realized at the time that most lay people receiving an invitation to a meeting on the C-B-D plan would not comprehend what the initials meant. There was, therefore, consternation and surprise when very few citizens turned out for a presentation on the city's heart—the central business district.

Meetings with clients (citizen advisory committees, policymakers, agency brass, grant givers, and so on) should be only when it's justified by the following conditions:

1. The clients have to make a decision (for example, more money is needed to do the project).
2. They have to know something to help them out of trouble.
3. There is a need to sort out possible misunderstandings.

Contingencies and Foul-Ups

In many organizations, the old army acronym SNAFU (situation normal, all fouled up) is essentially true because of the nature of the organization.[3]

Some observers state that more and more of the really large bureaucracies are beyond the capacity of any given individual to comprehend and, therefore, probably unmanageable.[4] Try, for example, to comprehend the organization chart of the U.S. Department of Housing and Urban Development (see Figure 4.3). Now you will possibly understand why handling SNAFUs is an art and not a science. Nevertheless, we fearlessly offer the following advice on coping with them, assuming your organization is not a similar bureaucratic swamp.

1. Don't cover up. Discuss the foul-ups openly and take responsibility for what happened.
2. Don't stay with things that don't work. Cut away fast and go on to something else. This was the lesson of the Viet Nam war.
3. Don't sucumb to complexosis. Doral Andrews defines this category of mental distress as,

   a disease of a mind that has been struggling too long in an ineffectual attempt to solve a complex problem. . .thought becomes circular brooding. The wheels are spinning, but not catching. . .What is done by those who can handle complexity over the long run is to take a break from consideration of the problem when the symptoms of indecisiveness and procrastination are extending. They take a vacation or the shorter-term forms of escapism giving the mind a rest from the problems.[5]

4. Negotiate for lower expectations: for example, the computer mapping system turns out unusable mush. Back to the drawing board to update the paper maps, then. People won't get maps out of an electronic slot, but from a human being which takes longer, but he or she is directly accountable, rather than through a software firm in Seattle.
5. Trim your losses and restore team morale. Failure is part of taking risks. It doesn't become a pattern after one crash.
6. Accept your losses and try to learn from them. Don't try to recapture them by cutting corners or cheating on the rest of the project. The value of the results will suffer, and you'll risk a bigger failure. Make sure you won't be caught by the same mistakes again.
7. You haven't failed if you tried your best and your project recommendations weren't understood or accepted. Don't try to own the problem, because you started working on it first. Remember all the people in history whose truth was ahead of its time. Try to substitute philosophy for frustration.
8. Even if the people you have to work with aren't what you really want or need, remember it's better to struggle with a sick donkey than to carry the wood yourself.

Figure 4.3. Organization chart, U.S. Department of Housing and Urban Development, 1966.

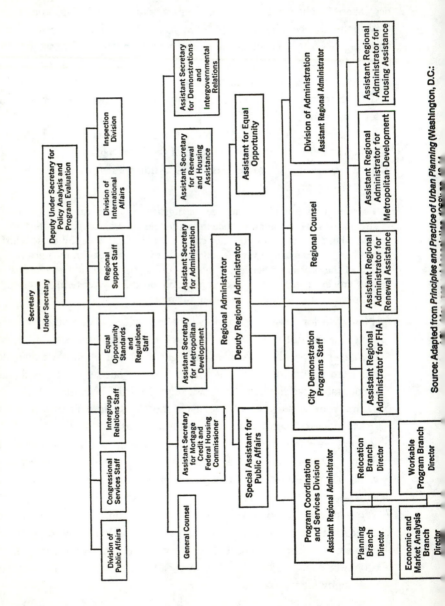

Source: Adapted from *Principles and Practice of Urban Planning* (Washington, D.C.:

A Crash Course in Budgeting Fundamentals

Will Rogers said, "We will never get anywhere with our finance till we pass a law saying that everytime we appropriate something, we got to pass a bill along with it stating where the money is coming from." The wave of taxpayer revolts has made Rogers' proposed law pretty much a rule in local government, where annual revenues control spending.

EVALUATING BUDGET PROPOSALS. One local budget review committee adopted the following criteria for evaluating annual budget proposals by various city bureaus:
1. Is this service one government needs to provide at X, Y, or Z levels?
2. Is this service being performed efficiently and effectively?
3. Is any additional increment of this service beyond a minimum base (the level below which the manager would not recommend continuing the function) worth what it will cost?
4. How is a particular program and its budget linked to citywide goals and objectives?
5. What will it cost to do next year? What was done this year? How does this sum compare with what will probably be available? This criteria which is known as "budget span" really asks how much of this year's level of service can be provided by next year's inflation-shrunken tax dollars and how will this be affected by a further squeeze on revenues from tax cuts, smaller federal and state subventions, higher pension and health benefit costs, and so on.

Bureau chiefs are now required to explain their budgets in these new terms; namely, what will be accomplished with any money they receive. Moreover, inflation deficits are treated as built-in budget cuts expressed as reductions in employment for most bureaus. What all this means to people further down the line is that all staff members should be able to assist in justifying their function, cost, and productivity.

In the past, many agencies simply presented line-item budgets, which were simply lists of various expenditures and this year's outlay was compared with next year's in such categories as travel, office supplies, salaries, furniture, and so on. A description of what was going to be produced or accomplished with the funds wasn't really available, and after some fiddling with inconsequentials, the status quo was generally approved, because tax money was abundant. Since then, budgets have increasingly been described in terms of programs and their products, and the results of doing the work or buying the capital projects. These budgets focus on the functions and tasks the department head recommends to be carried out. This format presents the policymaker with clearer choices than the traditional budget which described costs in terms of bureaus, and sections, people, and pencils. It's really a statement of what everyone on the payroll is going to accomplish and why. Nothing is taken for granted, simply because it was done last year.

Preparing such a budget should involve a task-force approach, so that the draftsman will estimate printing and graphics needs and costs, rather than a section chief. This budget should aim at optimizing the use of scarce resources. It should recognize competing demands and lean toward getting optimization through mixes, rather than if *A*, then not *B*. Politicians favor mixes over hard choices between options. The ideal is expressed in the 1979 Federal program mix—something for everybody, but less than anyone wanted. Thus, program *A* may be stretched out, while program *B* can be cut, but saved by shifting some of its funding to user fees.

THE PROGRAM BUDGET PROCESS. Money is the link here between various options. The staff must analyze each activity or program in terms of their contributions to policy objectives. Therefore, some priority choices must be ranked. (See Table 4.1.) There is a tendency for a staff to choose what it can do against what a broader view would choose as the most cost effective. Thus a department might want to expand its staff to handle a federally funded study, but in terms of cost-effectiveness, it might be better not to assume the front-end costs of getting more space or overcrowding existing space, hiring people who often begin to leave prior to the completion of the project, and so on. Thus, from a cost-effectiveness standpoint, it might be better to have a consultant do the production work of the study.

A determination of how given objectives can be obtained with minimum expenditure of resources must be made. First, a projection of output in terms of cases handled per year, families housed, number of children swimming in the city pool's summer program, or whatever functions are reasonably measurable in terms of a unit cost on the agency's budget. Then a social value can be put on the product—violations of city code to be removed, low income families to be decently housed, or probable reduction of delinquency. The U.S. Army Corps of Engineers, for example, uses the value of property saved from damage as a criterion.

These benefits are compared with costs over time (for example, building a low-income housing project versus administering rent supplements). The costs should not only include start-up and construction, but operat-

Table 4.1. A Sample Program Budget For a Planning Department

I. Contracted & Mandated Functions:	Costs:	Priority Rank*	Duration
a. Development Review	$162,000	1 (Volume controlled by outside functions)	Continuous
b. Zoning Enforcement	16,500	2 (Volume controlled by outside functions)	Continuous
c. Agricultural Preserves	47,300	1 (Volume controlled by outside functions)	Continuous
d. Housing Element Preparation	25,000	1 State legal reguirement for next year	1979-80
II. Essential Functions			
a. Public Information	$ 11,500	2 (Volume controlled by outside factions)	Continuous
b. Preparation of Development Ordinances	25,500	2 Needed to replace obsolete ordinances	1979-81
c. Traffic Study	12,000	1 Needed for use of road fund money	1979-80
d. Preparation for 1980 census	20,000	1 Essential for using data gathered by 1980 census	1979-80
III. Desirable Activities			
a. Civic Center Plan	22,000	3 Requested by City Council in 1978	1979-80
b. General Research and Education Data Bank	9,000	2	1979-80
c.	7,500	3 Final Phase of Revising Assessor's File for Use by Department	1979-80
d. Neighborhood Code Enforcement	10,000 (matching fund)	2 Awaiting Federal Action on Grant Annual Report	1980 est.
e. Publications	7,500	3 Information reports	1979-80
f. Area Plan for Kinneyville	11,000	2 Requested by Neighborhood Council	1979-81

*1 = Highest and compulsory   2 = Not recommended for deferral, but reduction possible   3 = Desirable if funds available.

ing and depreciation costs. Long-range project benefits are usually discounted at capital rate of return in the government bond market, and future costs are either stated in constant dollars or adjusted for inflation. Currently, inflation is a powerful determinant in making decisions about new capital projects and programs. For example, a new home in the San Francisco Bay area rose an average of 13.5 percent per year between 1967 and 1978, a rate much steeper than the cost-of-living index climb of 7.7 percent. Often decisions on capital improvements are made on the basis of getting them started before inflation puts them out of reach.

Alternatives and the impacts of each alternative must be prepared. For example, reducing the amount of public information given out over the phone and putting the callers on hold, as some airlines do, would save some clerical position costs, but it would also reduce daily contact with citizens and increase government's image as unresponsive.

Finally functions must be classified in terms of their flexibility for reduction, postponement, or elimination.

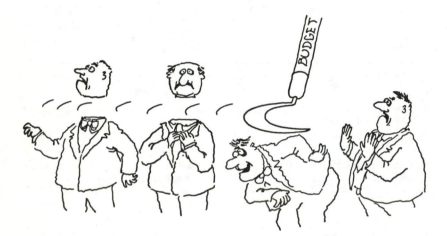

Decisionmaking: Developing Good Judgment

Anyone who allocates resources or time, offers advice, or implements policy is an executive. All executives face the problem of making the right decisions on what they themselves or others should do. Many people think that decisions are always made at the top. However, it is not just the executives at the top who face the problems of making decisions, for not all decisions are big ones. For example, you may face a decision on what to do about regulating and punishing the owners of housing built without permits. Use the following steps to help make decisions that tap your best judgmental powers:

1. *Do your homework first.* What principle or rule should your decision establish? Do you want to have all illegal houses decriminalized, penalized, or merely forced to be brought up to code?

2. *What are the limits of the decision?* Do you want the rule to apply only to whole structures or to illegal additions as well? Will new violators

be treated the same as predecision violators? Who will be involved in the impacts of your decision? How will they be affected?

3. *Think about what is right—first in terms of what are the best results you could establish in improving the situation.* Leave compromises, concessions, and political assessments for later on. Thus, you may decide that the best result for regulating illegal residences is not to punish them, per se, but to require them to rent to low income residents after bringing them up to code. Don't settle for what is merely adequate.

4. *You now need to develop the means to implement your decision.* Illegal homes, for example, could be brought up to code by using low-interest housing rehabilitation loans. This would actually improve the value of the owner's property and make the action more acceptable. That's the carrot. The stick could be the code power to fine or to order the work done when owners do not comply.

5. *Circulate the decision and get feedback from others who have special knowledge or a stake in the decision.* Evaluate this feedback and prepare some options and fallback positions. Be sure your tactics for gaining approval have feasible alternatives. This requires a strategy that is sufficiently flexible so that the decision can emerge from the heat of the political process reshaped, but unbroken.

6. *Finally, know your decisionmaking style.* Barry Phegan[6] noted that there are three main styles in management. (These are stereotypes, since very few people are totally one type to the exclusion of all others.)

- *The rational manager* believes that decisions are generated by information and solutions by analysis, that the essential problems are technical and rational, and that decisions are made *for* others. A desirable result will improve decisionmaking.

- *The action manager* believes that decisions are generated by pressures and that solutions come from action now, with such action being self-correcting through response to such actions. Essential problems are political, and power and decisions are made *through* others. A desirable result will resolve the issue.

- *The participatory manager* believes that decisions are generated by values and perceptions, and solutions, through discussions and inquiries. The essential problem is a psychological conflict of values and perceptions, and decisions are made with others. A desirable result will "help the client."

If your style differs from the other managers, the policymakers, or your co-workers, be patient, flexible, and very sure you know where the others are coming from, because their styles may be very hard to comprehend from your vantage point.

Managing Paperwork

People in government commonly complain that they're swamped with paperwork. But paper doesn't have to swamp you if you are aware of some of the ways to keep it from eating into your time.

1. Delegate authority to send notes, memos, and letters to anyone who can write intelligently. Don't be one of those channels everything in writing must go through.
2. If you're asked to review something, don't nit-pick. Write briefly in the margins, rather than composing a memo or book report as you did for the professor back in school.
3. Send correspondence and copies only to those with a valid need to know.
4. Does every project really need to be memorialized by a big fat report? Why not try a skinny one, backed by a fat file, from which copies can be sent to those exceptional people who like fat in their reading. Why not allow the report to really report, rather than induce sleep? The dictionary says the verb *report* means to record or present (a matter referred for consideration) with conclusions and recommendations. A good report should have the following characteristics:

- A short title should explain the purpose of the report.
- A summary should tell about the results of the work. This is the place for any recommendations. (If possible, a specific course of action should be recommended as opposed to further study.)
- The introduction should state as clearly as possible what the report is about.
- The main text takes the reader through the reasoning of the report in logical steps. (Do not detour through the history of the subject,

minutia about methodology used, and long tables of the statistics analyzed.)

- The conclusion should be a summary of where the logic of the report ends up in terms of what to do and why.
- Appendixes, exhibits, and other report fatteners should only be bound into the report for general distribution if there is a compelling reason.

Perhaps the worst propogators of thick, undigestable reports were the Environmental Impact Statement producers. The epitaph for this kind of paperwork was described in the following news-story leadline: "Agencies Fail to Use Studies."

> For the past nine years federal agencies have written "environmental impact statements" on proposed actions and then, all too often, ignored them in making the final decisions, says the President's Council on Environmental Quality.
>
> Now, backed by an executive order from President Carter, the Council has replaced its 5-year old "guidelines" with a set of mandatory regulations aimed at making the agencies take their own environmental studies seriously. . .
>
> At the same time, the new regulations seek to shorten and improve the environmental statements themselves. . . .the three member Council on Environmental Quality, responsible for reviewing environmental statements, became convinced that many statements were only paperwork, ignored by decision makers or written only to support decisions which had already been made. . . .
>
> Furthermore, it said, "the environmental impact statement has tended to become an end in itself, rather than a means to making better decisions. . . . In too many cases bulky EIS's have been prepared and transmitted, but not used by the decision maker."
>
> The Council's solution was a sweeping revision of the rules. Here are some major changes. . . .
> - Future studies must focus on all reasonable alternatives, comparing their environmental impacts clearly and seeking to *limit their length to a manageable 150–300 pages.*
> - The agency must publish a record showing how the environmental study was used in reaching its final decision.[7]

It might improve things to require all agencies to make public how they've used any study costing over $1,500.

MEMOS AND OTHER JUNK. Memos are the tools of coordination and protective coverage in most agencies. As such, they should be clear, concise, and state what kind of response or action is wanted from the recipients. As coordinating tools, they should inform others about something or should get a response by telling:

1. How to do something or why something needs not be done.
2. What was done when and with whom.
3. How to check out things before going ahead.
4. Why changes should be or were made in something.
5. What can be done now that we are running out of money, time, or supplies for a project.
6. Additional facts, which were forgotten earlier that you now think needs further explanation.

Memos can also be used as protection and can get others to share responsibility.

1. By noting what was said at a meeting, and to justify an action where you may be held accountable later on, for example, a memo of a conversation will cover you when a citizen comes in with a complaint. You say you'll look into it and report back on what can be done. However, the citizen later gripes to your boss that you promised to solve his problem then. (Note that all difficult people should get copies of memos of conversations.)
2. To document the position, facts, sources, and so on, on a topic you'll probably get back to later on, for example, when a project has proved to be a disaster as you forecast.
3. To note that you were authorized, ordered, or directed to do something by higher ups.

Junk That Should be Thrown Away. This type of material usually clutters up the files forever, because everyone's afraid to destroy public property. Therefore, consider the following guidelines to records management:

1. Rough drafts, first typed drafts, sketches, calculator tapes, and other materials that went into studies and reports long since completed or never completed.
2. Extra copies of notices, letters, memos, staff reports, agendas. These are generally stuck in the files to molder long after there's any need for them.
3. Correspondence, forms, minutes, and documents relating to projects abandoned, denied, never started, or closed out over three years ago. Put what needs to be kept for posterity on microfilm, or in archive storage. Files should always be thined out before being stored.

NOTES

1.   The best technique, once you've got a fixed date, is to construct a work program calendar that begins with that date and works backward to the date the work starts. If that is 32 weeks, then systematically lay out the number of weeks required for each task, being sure to apply rigor to getting each task done on time. For two decades of our lives, while in school, we learned to ignore or play games with this sort of reality and to put production off until the last moment. This habit must be unlearned quickly and replaced with a workable schedule.

2.   This is not to be confused with Parkinson's "Law of Delay," which states, "Delay is the deadliest form of denial." The ploy of "letting the dinosaurs die off" avoids the types who thought about the problem by sending out for "more study." It also allows the "abominable no men" to be identified and bypassed or outvoted in due time. Sending a project into a policy-making group whose majority is made up of decision avoiders is to send it up prematurely.

3.   Thomas L. Martin, Jr. in his book, *Malice in Blunderland* (New York: McGraw–Hill, 1973), has gathered some of the satirical management theories that apply here. A sampling would be:
Jones's Law (anonymous): "The man who can smile when things go wrong has thought of someone he can blame it on" (p. 25). Finagle's Laws (anonymous): "The likelihood of a thing happening is inversely proportional to its desirability" (p. 10). And once a job is fouled up anything done to improve it only makes it worse."

4.   "Modern society must face up to the prospect that we may be reaching the limits of our capacity to manage exceedingly large and complex bureaucracies. . . . Indeed, there is growing concern whether many of the largest bureaucracies can survive." Duane S. Elgin and Robert A. Bushnell, "The Limits to Complexity: Bureaucracies Becoming Unmanageable?", *Futurist,* December 1977, p. 337.

5.   Jack McCarthy, "Complexitosis, A Paralysis of the Mind," *Northwest Magazine, Oregonian* (Portland, Oregon) May 21, 1978, p. NW2.

6.   Barry Phegan, "Characteristics of the Three Basic Management Styles" (Berkeley, California: Pacific Management Group, 1976).

7.   Stan Benjamin, "Agencies Fail to Use Studies," *Oregonian* (Portland, Oregon), January 4, 1979, p. A8. © The Associated Press.

R.H. 80

Chapter Five
Knowing What You Are
Doing, Why, and
for Whom

Peter's theory of relevant knowledge:
Ignorance is no excuse—it's the real thing.

—Laurence J. Peter*

This book has concentrated on the skills necessary to everyone on the road to a satisfying career in local government. Chapter 6 will attempt to indicate paths any entry-level person, regardless of discipline or profession, should follow in order to advance smoothly and prepare for lifetime career and job satisfaction. But, the reader should not overlook the importance of subject content, basic knowledge, and generalist or technical skills concerning the field in which he or she practices. Knowing what needs doing and the substance of your agency's or institution's mission is important, too. In fact, while we stress how to approach and do a job effectively, and how to advance careers and create job satisfaction, it is well to be reminded, too, that most of us are directly or indirectly in the public's employ. Our jobs involve carrying out a *public* purpose or objective and providing a *public* service. We need to know what these objectives and services are and what methods and strategies should be employed to achieve necessary and meaningful results. We also need to know the whys of the job and for whom we are working and being paid.

*Laurence J. Peter, *San Francisco Chronicle*, February 18, 1979.

GETTING IN TOUCH WITH WHAT YOU KNOW

Whether your background is in economics, urban planning, public policy analysis, public health, social welfare, outdoor recreation, forestry, or public land management, you are bound to have some conception of and familiarity with the body of knowledge in your field. If you came into a field by accident, that is, without a formal educational background or training, you have a real advantage over the recent college graduate whose sole familiarity with the field is derived from the classroom and textbooks. You know from experience what is practical and workable, who has the power, where the money is, and how to get things done. However, you may be unaware of how much a disadvantage it is to be "on the front line" and, therefore, far removed from why you are doing what you are doing. You may be shortchanging yourself and your client for lack of any real understanding of the basic values and policy issues underlying your agency's tasks. Like the helmsman of a ship at sea, you may be doing a splendid job carrying out the limited assignment of holding to a set course and yet getting too preoccupied to notice that perhaps the direction of the ship is aimed straight at the rocks, or that perhaps the entire trip is poorly thought-out or ill-conceived. Worse yet, you might not have been able to discover why you are doing the task assigned or whether doing it well makes any difference within the larger overall scheme of things.

In short, in addition to developing working, scheduling, production, communication, and management skills (process skills transferable to virtually any line of work, profession, or field), you have an obligation to

know what to do and why you are doing it, and for whose benefit. Every now and then consider reassessing how knowledgeable you are about the subject or problem you deal with regularly. If you feel inadequate, out of date, or long on experience and short on theory, maybe it is time to do something about it. Your professional growth plan will be discussed in chapters 6 and 7.

In the meantime, here are a few pointers on how to get a fix on the basic professional or technical knowledge you need while on the job.

Go directly to your agency or organization's act of creation. Whether it's a charter, legislative act, ordinance, or organizational by-laws, it sets forth the organization's reason for being, its purposes, objectives, and mandates. As the principal frame of reference, it should give you a definite sense of mission and an understanding of why you are assigned to do what you are doing.

In your own mind, assess whether the "act of creation" is adequate and relevant. Maybe it is, but maybe it is not broadly enough conceived, or maybe it fails to recognize current realities. How can you be sure? One answer is to read a great deal of the current literature in your subject field (include such sources as books, journal articles, current criticisms in daily newspapers, and so on). Try to grasp a sense of history and theory as the basis for deciding whether your agency is "on the cutting edge" or just coasting along. With your grasp of theory (what could and ought to be), you should have no trouble evaluating your agency's mission and performance. In the process, you will have increased your knowledge and understanding and even readied yourself, perhaps, for more responsibility or a better job.

Examine the legislation, regulations, policies, mandates, and guidelines that bear on your client's or your agency's responsibilities. You must be able to cite all of them and understand how you can or must draw on them as part of your own responsibilities. Many people work in places where carrying out either directly or indirectly a federal or state mandate is the essence of the job. This requires an understanding of the rules and their application. You will also need to know how to secure available funds for the benefit of the client agency or organization. This process of self-learning is bound to expand your knowledge and your marketability as well as your service to your client.

Continually evaluate your underlying values and assumptions. This can be hard to do. It's easy to be a "true believer," or to accept dogma readily. Some people never raise fundamental questions, continuing to believe in established values in the face of unremitting change, or they change ideas too readily when to do so actually may be premature or contrary to obvious or well-established evidence or values. But, proceeding boldly in the wrong direction for the wrong reasons is a human shortcoming. Those of us in public service particularly need to carefully evaluate our own behavior to be sure our own values and objectives are not causing policy directions to be followed which might in the long run be unfortunate or disastrous.

There is much current reference to the phrase "beware of the expert" simply because the so-called experts often have been skilled at getting things done. Often these same experts lack the skill to ask themselves and others what ought to be done, whether it ought to be done, and what alternatives are available and are indicated by the circumstances. Urban renewal in some American cities is the story of having moved insensitively and thoughtlessly in an efficient and well-organized manner. Asking and knowing how to deal with these questions is the sign of a knowledgeable and thoughtful public servant or professional. If you don't know how to deal with the questions, or if there is no time, your client suffers and so do you.[1]

Take advantage of opportunities to study and examine what others are doing, the latest methods of analysis, mapmaking, or simply to brush up on theory and current developments in the law. We cannot afford to be limited to our impulses or convictions that we know what is right. Self-renewal is essential to ensure continuing motivation, understanding, sensitivity, and creativity.

Lawyers and other business executives readily allocate time and money for continuing education for both themselves and those who work for them. While the local and state public sector in large part finds it defensible only in good times and even then only on a limited scale and for a few persons once in a while.

WHO IS THE CLIENT?

One of the stickier puzzles for the newly appointed public servant is trying to figure out who the client is. You may think it is your immediate supervisor, the person who directs and holds some direct power over your future. And so on up the line. In a line agency, this may be so; but even a police officer must be conscious that the job is to satisfy not only the sergeant but also the victim of a crime, the general public, the ACLU

(American Civil Liberties Union) the courts (if there's litigation), and the police review board, while also recognizing the rights of the accused. Even in a quasi-military organization, more than one client exists. This makes the job tougher, the demands on you greater, and the need for education (generalist skills) and training (specialist and other) skills very essential.

When undertaking a task, one ought to compose a complete list of clients for whom you are working, their expectations, and their role in a project's planning, programming, management, decisionmaking, or implementation.

Ethical Standards

One of the problems of public employment at all levels of government is that the rules for telling right from wrong are not always clear—although most of us think it quite clear when a wrong is done by someone else. It is not enough to say we always act or should act professionally. What does this mean? The question has resulted in substantial soul-searching for many planners, administrators, and specialists both inside and outside public agencies. In fact, in some cases, specific legal opinions have even been made with respect to so-called conflicts of interest. But other problems prevail, and ethical standards are not always clear, internally consistent, broadly respected, or enforced.

Obligations to clients often conflict with obligations to the public. For example, your client, narrowly defined, may be the elected body that hired you, while the public may very well have different expectations. And there may be various publics. What do you do to reconcile the differences? This may be a question of ethics. Following professionally accepted standards of conduct may produce results not to the public's liking. A professional society's responsibility may be to serve and protect its members, even at the expense of the public's expectations that professional conduct ought to be judged by the public itself. Where do you stand on this issue? For example, should licensing boards be composed of the regulated or of lay members capable of judging the conduct of the licensed?

Peter Marcuse lays out still another dilemma neatly:

> The social scientist's role creates ethical obligations for the planner—and ethical ambiguities—very much as the economist's role does for the fiscal

advisor, or the chemist's for the weapon's expert. In each case, the scientific role calls for dedication to the pursuit of knowledge for its own sake, without regard to where it may lead; caution and complete exploration of all facets before arriving at conclusions; full disclosure of methods and results; in other words, the discovery and dissemination of the truth. The planner acting as planner, however, may have quite different, and often conflicting, ethical obligations: to act decisively in accordance with a client's timetable, subject to the client's priorities; to consider the practical impact of disclosures and findings; to economize in the pursuit of alternatives; to be responsible for ultimate products.[2]

So, what is there beyond professional ethics, assuming as Marcuse does that they alone do not at present serve us well? In short, professional ethics in planning—and he is limiting himself to planners—merits much more attention than it has received. A clear statement of how planners, administrators, and other professionals and public servants should conduct themselves "requires looking beyond professional ethics to the functions the profession serves, the tasks it is assigned. If a given task is harmful, executing it is not desirable."

Each person entering public service shares the obligation to try to work under a body of ethical standards. These standards are designed to ensure fairness, due process, and loyalty and service to the clients, as well as service to the various publics being served by the public agency without sacrificing service to and respect for the public good and social responsibility. If they don't already exist, formulate your own.

NOTES

1. The Viet Nam war experience was also the quintessence of misguided minds in the public service. Those "experts" led a whole society down the wrong path for the wrong reasons. And, to make it worse, they excelled in the process skills of communication, organization, scheduling, and management.

2. Peter Marcuse, "Professional Ethics and Beyond: Values in Planning," *Journal of the American Institute of Planners,* July 1976, p. 269.

Taking stock

Chapter Six
Making and
Implementing
a Career Plan

*If you don't know where you are going,
you will end up somewhere else.*

—Laurence J. Peter*

All individuals who enter service in either a public agency or private group as planners, community development or transportation specialists, project or program administrators, administrative assistants, employees in community or social service agencies, or other employees or aspirants for jobs in public agencies probably have the following things on their minds:

1. *Will the job I take satisfy me?* Salary, vacation, working hours, compatibility with co-workers, freedom and opportunity to work independently and make decisions, office amenities, and the character and intrinsic value of the work to be performed—all must be considered in answering this question.

2. *Will the job lead to something better?* Most of us want to be promoted, take on more responsibility, make more money, and gain recognition from our peers and society. Each job up the ladder of success should fulfill our need to progress towards our own personal and professional goals.

3. *Am I prepared?* There is bound to be some uncertainty when entering a new profession and accepting a first job. Do I have the proper education and background? Do I have the required skills? What do the

---

*The Peter Principle is "In a hierarchy, each employee tends to rise to his or her level of incompetence." Laurence J. Peter and Raymond Hull, *The Peter Principle, Why Things Go Wrong* (New York: William Morrow, 1965).

people who are selecting new employees expect me to know and be able to do? Is there a good match between their expectations and my capabilities?

4. *Will they like me?* If I am satisfied on the first three counts, and confident about my readiness for the job, I may wonder, nevertheless, whether the situation will be right. One can only speculate about the suitability of one's clothes, hair style, and personality; but these are legitimate concerns.

5. *Will I be able to do a good job?* Assuming I'm hired, will I be able to do the job both I and my new employer believe I can do? Are there some skills I lack? Did I oversell myself? Can I learn rapidly on the job or by taking a night course? Will the demands of the job overwhelm me and exceed my capabilities?

All of these are legitimate questions. Everyone is bound to be puzzled by such concerns when starting up the career ladder. For many, contemplating or undertaking the first job is a stressful experience, mostly because of the uncertainties suggested by these five questions. However, much of the answer lies within yourself.

So, let us take stock of who you are, where you are going, what capabilities you possess, and what skills you must develop to gain personal satisfaction, perform effectively, and enjoy your career.

MAKING AN INDIVIDUAL PLAN

Step One: Taking Stock of Yourself

The first thing to do is look at yourself and find answers to the following questions: What are your skills? Select from the list of common skills required in local government (see Table 6.1). Consider the skills you possess, prefer, can do but don't want to be stuck with, and those you actively dislike. (This list may be expanded to include skills particular to your training and background.)

Which skills are you attracted to? Remember, you cannot be expected to be competent in all areas. However, you are likely to do best and enjoy the work the most if you are doing what you are attracted to. Some people like to do research, while others enjoy managing projects or an agency. Others prefer to work with the public in a community setting. Do you know for sure about your own likes and dislikes?

Table 6.1. Skills Often Required
in Local Government

	Skills I Have and Enjoy	Skills I Have But Don't Enjoy	Skills I Want to Learn	Skills I Probably Should Have But Am Not Too Enthusiastic About Learning
Generalist Skills				
Researches				
Recognizes need for information and how to get it.				
Adept at interviewing and survey research				
Researches exhaustively and collects usable data				
Disects and analyzes information				
Diagnoses problems				
Classifies information and data				
Traces problems to their source				
Deals systematically with large amount of information				
Measures and evaluates objectively				
Presents findings cogently				
Identifies problems, issues, and goals				
Considers alternative courses of action				
Determines what needs to be done, why, and for whom				
Develops priorities				
Others (list)				
Specialist Skills				
Depends upon your area of specialization. Items to be filled in by person completing this exercise.				
1.				
2.				
3.				

	Skills I Have and Enjoy	Skills I Have But Don't Enjoy	Skills I Want to Learn	Skills I Probably Should Have But Am Not Too Enthusiastic About Learning

New Technology Skills

Depends upon your areas of specialization and interest. Items to be filled in by person completing this exercise.

1.

2.

3.

Social-Personal Skills

Copes effectively with stress

Copes with difficult people

Fosters interpersonal relations

Handles client services and is responsive to client needs

Others (list)

Communication Skills

Writes memos and reports in jargon-free, clean English

Drafts, draws, and otherwise communicates graphically or with visual aids.

Speaks well before the public

Is adept at facilitating dialogue in meetings

Gives and follows directions

Runs a meeting well

Works well with the public

Others (list)

Work Programming and Management Skills

Designs programs that work well; coordinates tasks and people, sets priorities

Manages time well (of self and others)

Shows organizational planning and development

Manages job or project well

Is effective leader and supervisor; helps others develop their own capacities

	Skills I Have and Enjoy	Skills I Have But Don't Enjoy	Skills I Want to Learn	Skills I Probably Should Have But Am Not Too Enthusiastic About Learning
Is adept at employee development and to orienting new people to the job and the agency				
Utilizes employees well and shows job satisfaction				
Delegates authority and responsibility				
Is adept at team building				
Is adept at budgeting and fiscal management				
Resolves conflicts by negotiating, brokering, and mediating				
Communicates with others; gives directions effectively				
Inspires loyalty				
Is able to make hard decisions				
Often continually strives to assume more responsibility				
Takes the initiative and gets things done with relative ease				
Others (list)				

Stylistic Skills

Shows good judgment

Has ability to command attention and respect

Shows patience

Is courteous and calm in the face of hostility

Is adept at selling new ideas

Is adept at facilitating the support of others

Shows sensitivity to the points of view, feelings, needs and values of others; is able to establish rapport

Is a good listener

Is diligent and energetic

Is assertive

Is fair and equitable

Is reasonable

	Skills I Have and Enjoy	Skills I Have But Don't Enjoy	Skills I Want to Learn	Skills I Probably Should Have But Am Not Too Enthusiastic About Learning
Is willing to take risks				
Perceives how things could be rather than accepting them as they are				
Recognizes opportunities and takes advantage of them				
Is self-directed				
Is tactful				

Other skills
List those skills you have or would like to acquire that are not already listed.

Specialist Skills
New Technology Skills
Social-Personal Skills

It's time to find out if you are searching or wondering about your career. While this book has emphasized the skills employers are looking for, it's just as important for you to decide what's good for you. This may be done by completing the exercise found in Table 6.1. Be honest with yourself in distinguishing between skills you now have and those you would like to acquire. Do not be afraid to acknowledge that some skills others might like you to have are not your cup of tea. Don't force yourself into computer programming if what you really prefer is community organizing or graphic design.

Step Two: Your Work Preferences or Goals

1. For what kinds of places would you like to work (for example, a small agency, a large one, or a nonagency?)
2. Where would you like to work (geographic place)?
3. What kind of work would suit you?
In order to evaluate yourself, you should identify what the characteristics of an ideal job are. You can use the exercise provided in Table 6.2.

Table 6.2. Setting Career Goals
and Achieving Them

Your Work Preference

Describe the kind of working environment you'd like to have in terms of the following:

1. The kinds of people you want to work with:

_____

_____

2. The working conditions you would prefer:

_____

_____

3. The ethics and values you want to have in your office:

_____

_____

4. The issues and problems you want to work on:

_____

_____

5. What you want to accomplish with your work:

_____

_____

6. The values and lifestyle that you wouldn't compromise for the sake of your job:

_____

_____

7. Your immediate and long-range financial needs or goals:

_____

_____

8. How you want to further develop your own skills and knowledge through job experience:

_____

_____

Now match up your work preferences with your existing skills and skill preferences and rough out your career plans. Include the following elements:

What I need now to improve my present situation is (circle your answer):

1. To improve in the job I now hold by
a. more training
b. responsibility
c. better or broader work experience
d. better working conditions
e. something else (describe) _____

2. To move up
3. To move out and get a better job (describe specifically what improvements you're looking for)
4. To get a job

Future Concerns

1. What I'd like to be working at in five years is (describe in terms of earlier

   answers): _____

   _____

2. What I expect to be working at in five years is _____

   _____

3. My greatest career disappointment would be to find myself five years from now in the following situation (describe in terms of earlier answers):

   _____

   _____

   _____

KNOW WHAT YOU WANT FROM A JOB

What Does it Take to Make You Happy on a Job? This is essential in learning what you want from a job. Researchers at the Alfred P. Sloan School of Management at MIT have claimed:

> How much satisfaction people get out of their jobs may have less to do with the actual work they perform than their total outlook on life. They believe that job success cannot be defined by income and achievement alone but by the balancing of individual, occupational, and family factors which vary throughout life. . .The idea that the job is "it" is unrealistic. . .and it leads to frustration on the employee's part, and inefficiency to the company.

Among the variables that impact on a person's career are "career anchors" which "reflect the motives, talents and values that people seek to express through their work. Job satisfaction depends on the extent that people and their employees understand these motives and create opportunities for their expression."

Five Career Anchors

1. *Managerial Competence.* Persons governed by this anchor are able to leave technical chores behind to function fully as managers. They are

motivated by a need to climb to a level of an organization where their own managerial behavior makes a real difference to the functioning of the organization.

2. *Technical-Functional Competence.* For these persons the need above all else is to exercise their technical talents. They will resist being promoted out of a technically satisfying job into one that is managerial even though they know that the American success model is to climb as high as possible.

3. *Security.* Some people are primarily motivated by the need to stabilize a career and will do whatever is required to maintain job security and a decent income.

4. *Creativity.* One of the more complex anchors. . . .these persons' main motive is the need to build or create something that is entirely their own product.

5. *Autonomy and independence.* Persons in this group—professors, teachers, private consultants—seek jobs that are maximally free of organizational constraints.

How can people increase job satisfaction?. . . .By deciding how their jobs fit into their total life space, by knowing what gives them the most satisfaction. The idea is not to separate life and work but to make them mesh together so the end result is not job satisfaction but life satisfaction.[1]

For the entry-level person, another "career anchor" might be the quality and diversity of experience one could get from a job. This is particularly important if you're not sure as yet which of the other five should govern your choice of where to look.

SHOULD I LOOK AT BIG OR SMALL ORGANIZATIONS?
Large organizations have greater promotional opportunities, more rapid advancement and more diversity in work experience for specialists or those who wish to specialize. For those who want to rise to managerial status, or find a niche in a technical specialty without spreading themselves thin, a large agency is probably the best place to select for the job hunt. A small organization offers more for people who value creativity and some greater degree of freedom from organizational impersonality and rules. For those who can accept greater responsibility, want to work closer to policymaking, or have a broader scope to their duties, the small agency is probably the best place to start.

SECURITY. These days, it's hard to say which kind of a place offers the best security. Since 80 percent or more of a city or county's budget is often in the form of the payroll, it is becoming more and more important to analyze the nature of the budget for the agency you might want to join. This is because budget cuts will necessarily mean reducing positions.

There are three major things to find out about the funding that might be the source of your paycheck.

1. Are you shipping out on the *Titanic?* Does the agency or program you would work with get its money from local sources or from outside (federal, state, foundation) sources? If it is local, learn how much commitment there was to the service you might provide. It could be that you might just be a stopgap to hold things together for the interim. The position may have become vacant because your predecessor decided not to stay to the end and the biggest responsibility you may have before your next job hunt is packing the project's files off to the archives. If the funding is from outside sources, you should also check to find out what stage of its life cycle the program may be entering. Is funding on an annual basis and dependent on whether Washington or some other remote place keeps the dollars coming for another year in the same amount? Once again, you may be stepping into the terminal phase of a once viable job. Do so only if you need survival money, and don't mind updating your resume.

2. Are you buying a lame duck? Is the program or agency you're joining controversial? Is its chief a political appointee? Is its life dependent on a bare majority or a strong politician? If the answer to any of these questions is *yes*, then you may find that you'll either be jobless after the next election or running the duplicator in the basement after the new administration's budget revisions take effect.

3. Are you dressed for a deep freeze? As inflation takes its toll, tax revolts simmer, and politicians run more and more scared, the hiring freeze becomes a favorite ploy. In such cases, know the circumstances surrounding the vacancy you may fill. Are positions filled only when turnover exceeds a certain rate? Is your position paid for by permit or user fees? What happens when business drops off? Your position may have been created by a temporary flare-up in building activity or some other ephemeral phenomenon. If any of these conditions prevail, seek such employment without illusions about security. Some people don't mind being white collar migrant workers, but if security and settling down are important to you, such jobs will cause stress and may lower your morale for the next job hunt.

Check your responses in six months and again one year from now. Are you getting anywhere? Have you changed your mind about what you want? Update your career plan whenever your circumstances change and evaluate where the change has taken you and what you can do about it.

Step Three: Matching Up Steps One and Two and Coming Up With a Career Plan

Now it is time for you to evaluate your likes and dislikes, your goals, and your skills. You have written down your goals and you have completed the inventory of skills. So consider this question: what combination of goals, skills, needs and preferences is right for you? Again, think about your total self and do not fall into the trap of separating your career from the rest of your life. When you complete this task, you will have the basis for a career plan: you will know what your goals are, what will make you happy, and what skills you have to offer. Undoubtedly the essence of your career plan is a combination of what to do and where to do it. But it is also building your bank of skills. In this regard, Richard Bolles' moral is worth remembering: "The higher skill level you can legitimately claim, the more likely you are to find a job."[2] The reason being that fewer people are competing for jobs requiring a high level of skills. If you are so skilled, you may be competing with practically no one else. You may even be able to create a brand new job for yourself in an organization, that is, once you persuade them of their needs.

The matching of all these elements together is your plan. But like any other planning, don't let the process stop there. Don't let an incomplete plan gather dust on the shelf. Set to paper the specific actions you will take to implement your plan.

Like most plans, yours may deserve to be scrapped as new events occur in your life or if you gain new insights about yourself. Don't worry about it. Since it's your plan, you need neither to defend a change of direction nor do you need to implement a plan that's wrong for you. But, if it is the right plan, respect it and stick to it.

IMPLEMENTING YOUR PLAN

Step One: The Search for Work

FINDING JOB OPENINGS.   The most complex and frustrating part of your career will be finding and getting a job. But the following can aid you in this process.

Publications.   You can find many publications that advertise jobs in the public sector in a university or municipal reference library:

Jobs Available in the Public Sector, P.O. Box 1040, Modesto, CA 95353; covers the Western states.

Jobs in Planning, published semi-monthly by the American Planning Association, 1313 E. 60th St., Chicago, IL 60637; covers the U.S. and some foreign countries.

The American City and County, Berkshire Common, Pittsfield, MA 01201

Public Administration Times, American Society for Public Administration, 1225 Connecticut Ave. N.W., Washington, D.C. 20036.

International City Management Association Newsletter, 1140 Connecticut Ave. N.W., Washington, D.C. 20036.

Journal of Housing, National Association of Housing and Redevelopment Officials, Suite 404, 2600 Virginia Ave. N.W., Washington, D.C. 20037.

Nation's Cities, National League of Cities, 1620 Eye St., N.W., Washington, D.C. 20036.

ITE Journal, Institute of Transportation Engineers, 1815 North Ft. Meyer Dr., Suite 905, Arlington, VA 22209.

There are also several excellent regional sources of job listings for local governments.

Municipal South, Clark Publishing Co., P.O. Box 88, Greenville, SC 29602.

Western City Magazine, League of California Cities, Hotel Claremont, Berkeley, CA 94705.

The Job Finder, Western Governmental Research Association, 109 Moses Hall, University of California, Berkeley, CA 94720.

Federal Bulletin (issued every three months) is available free at local offices of personnel management.

Other Leads. Almost every state has a publication put out by the state league of cities or municipal league.

Personal referrals can come from friends, professors, university place-ment officers, or other classmates who are already employed or actively looking. Your college alumni association may be able to match you with a job in your field or in an agency where you would like to work.

Finally, if you don't mind long waits, there's the local state employ-ment office which in many areas has very current and complete files of public service jobs.

APPLYING FOR WORK. Let's assume you've located a lead that seems to offer you a chance to work at something you would like to do. You should always check to see that you're not wasting your time on one of those cretinous agencies that rob job seekers of valuable time and effort by committing one of the following:

1. Short-fuse deadlines which make it almost impossible for the applicant to apply by mail.

2. Pro forma ads which simply build up the personnel files and show compliance with affirmative action regulations, when the agency fully intends to fill the vacancy in house.

3. Intelligence insulting forms with questions like: "Are you flexible enough to quickly adjust to changes in workload and deadlines?" or "Do you have a complete knowledge of budgetary and administrative docu-ments and procedures regarding staffing and programming?" This includes a knowledge of revenue sources, requirements for receipts, and funds for other departments. Describe fully your knowledge and experi-ence below. The "below" is often a box measuring ¼" by 6". In defense of this practice, one personnel analyst revealed to the authors that such things are deliberate rather than mindless in order to reveal whether the applicant can follow directions explicitly. When you see questions like this, look elsewhere on the form for permission to add supplementary sheets as necessary. The general idea of application forms, however, is to see if you wash out on paper. Some hints from personnel people on how to avoid these entrapments include:

a. *Follow directions carefully.* For example, when you are asked for a description of the duties and responsibilities of your last job, write or type them on the form. Do not print "See resume on file." (For practice try doing Can You Follow Directions, Figure 6.1.)

b. *Reason for leaving.* Be very honest about your last two or three jobs.

Figure 6.1. Can You Follow Directions

1. Read everything carefully before doing anything.
2. Put your name in the upper right hand corner of this page.
3. Circle the word "NAME" in sentence number 2.
4. Draw five small squares in the upper left hand corner.
5. Put an "X" in each square.
6. Put a circle around each square.
7. Sign your name under the title of this paper.
8. After the title, write, "Yes, yes, yes."
9. Put a circle completely around sentence number 7.
10. Put an "X" in the lower left corner of this page.
11. Draw a triangle around the "X" you have just put down.
12. On the back of this paper, multiply 703 by 66.
13. Draw a rectangle around the word "CORNER" in sentence four.
14. Loudly call out your first name when you get this far along.
15. If you have followed directions carefully to this point, call out, "I have."
16. On the reverse side of this paper, add 8950 and 9805.
17. Put a circle around your answer and put a square around the circle.
18. In your normal speaking voice, count from 10 to 1 backwards.
19. Punch three small holes in the top of this paper with your pen or pencil point.
20. If you are the first person to reach this point, loudly call out, "I am the first person to reach this point and I AM THE LEADER at following directions."
21. Underline all even numbers on the left side of this paper.
22. Loudly call out. "I AM NEARLY FINISHED. I HAVE FOLLOWED DIRECTIONS."
23. Now that you have finished reading everything carefully, do only sentences one and two.

Source: Sonoma County Personnel Department, 1975.

Often the personnel people will check with past employers or supervisors before giving you an interview. It doesn't help to bad mouth a former employer, even though the criticism may be richly deserved.

c. *Don't state your salary requirements right off.* While most government jobs are bracketed within a given range, the step levels are frequently negotiable after you've been offered the job. Even if salary requirements are requested, it's usually impolitic to state a demand before you know you're wanted.

Once you've checked out your leads, you will want to send a resume and cover letter to the more promising ones. The important thing to remember about these is that their main purpose is to get you an interview.

RESUMES. The optimum length is one to two pages. Act as if you are sending a telegram, for many vacancies in today's tight job market will attract over 100 responses. The main things to list are all the basic activities and skills you have acquired in recent employment. (You can never be sure of what they're looking for.) For recent graduates, it helpts to put your educational record first especially if you have an impressive record (awards, scholarships, grants, honors) but little employment experience. Stress your essential qualifications for the job.

References are a precious resource to be hoarded until you're really being seriously considered for the job. After all, you're asking them to volunteer their time on your behalf and filling out forms for personnel clerks gets to be a pain—fast! Always ask permission to use someone's name for a reference.

Listing previous salaries on a resume could either make the prospective employers reduce what they were going to offer or make them think you're too high priced.

Don't list hobbies. They only clutter up a resume and they're also irrelevant.

Don't include photographs, since they are often an embarrassment.

Don't put career objectives on a resume. If you really believe that such things will help you sell yourself to a prospective employer, compose them in terms applicable to a specific job in the cover letter.

Slick typeset resumes or professionally composed ones can all too often turn a prospective employer off. Use your own words and get clean copies of a typed version. More than one version may be helpful. For example, a resume for an academic or research position should stress training, publications and professional presentations, teaching research, and so on, while a professional looking for work in a government agency should stress skills and abilities relevant to the demands of the vacancy. *Remember* the purpose of the resume is to get you invited to an interview.

COVER LETTERS. Since cover letters are frequently more important than the resume, they should be geared to what you think the needs are of the place you'd like to work.

Focus three to four paragraphs on the special qualifications you have that don't fit within the format of the resume. If possible, do a little homework on the agency and mention how you might fill a need that wasn't mentioned in the job ad.

This is the place to mention why you want to come and work for this particular place in this particular job and what you can do for them.[3] This will often come up in an interview so make sure you have clearly thought it out.

Step Two: Be Aware of Some Recent Trends in Government Hiring.

There seems to be an increasing trend in many agencies to stress skills, rather than credentials, such as degrees, professional memberships, years of experience and former job titles. Some personnel people say that some of this stems from affirmative action policies, but more of it seems to be a reflection of unhappy experience with university graduates who weren't up to par. For example, a West Coast city requires applicants to fill out forms such as the one shown in Figure 6.2 for the position of City Planner II. Note that applicants have to list "the specific work, education, or training experiences that have enabled you to acquire the knowledge or skill." Later on, those that claim to have the required skills or knowledge will be tested on *how well* they can apply these attributes to situations that might arise on the job. The moral of this trend is simple. Be sure you know what you claim to know and can apply your knowledge to work situations.[4]

The final word on the myths that persist on job hunting was written by Julie Monson, an assistant director of placement at Pomona College.[5]

Figure 6.2. A Typical Application Form Based on Qualifications

I.D. Number_____

SECTION V
City Planner II
SUPPLEMENTAL INFORMATION

READ THESE INSTRUCTIONS CAREFULLY.

The purpose of this supplemental application form is to obtain detailed information regarding your qualifications for this position. This information will be used to screen applicants for this examination. This form must be filled out completely. Information must be supplied in the format of this form. PREPARED RESUMES WILL NOT BE CONSIDERED.

Pages 1 through 4 of this form list Minimum Qualifications required of all applicants. Persons applying for this job *must have* the Minimum Qualifications that are listed. Check "YES" or "NO" for each Minimum Qualification. For each "YES" answer, list the appropriate Education Code number from Section II of the application and/or the Work Code letter from Section IV. Additionally, for each "YES" answer, list the specific work, education, or training experiences that have enabled you to acquire the knowledge or skill. Be specific in your answers; List the specific courses, job assignments, degree of your responsibility, size and scope of project, amount of supervision received, number and titles of persons you supervised, etc.

Pages 5 through 6 of this form identify specialized discipline areas that *may* be taught on the job. We are hoping to find candidates who are now qualified in these areas. Each candidate may complete as many or none of these discipline areas as he/she chooses.

REMEMBER: Candidates will be given specialty tests *only* in those specialty areas they responded to in this section and passed based on a review of the application.

Check "YES" or "NO" for each of these disciplines. For each "YES" answer, list the appropriate Education Code number or Work Code letter in the space provided. Then supply specific information for each "YES" answer as you did for the Minimum Qualifications.

City Planner II
SUPLEMENTAL APPLICATION FORM
Minimum Qualifications

Yes ☐ No ☐   Basic knowledge of a wide range of planning issues, concerns, and methodologies applied in an urban setting. Includes development and analysis of alternative policies and plans to guide urban development decisions in areas such as economics, land use, transportation, urban design, neighborhood planning and manpower planning.

Yes ☐ No ☐   Skill in information and data collection and analysis. Includes use of primary and secondary source data, comparison and analysis of codes, rules, regulations, legal documents and grant and budget specifications. Please indicate type of data or information used and purpose for which analysis was done.

Yes ☐ No ☐   Skill in translating and explaining technical matters to
                a lay audience. Includes both writing procedural and
                explanatory brochures or papers and presenting
                information orally.

Yes ☐ No ☐   Skill in preparing clear, concise working papers and
                technical documents and presenting information in
                written form. Includes writing reports, technical
                memoranda, ordinances, articles and grant applications.

TRANSPORTATION

Yes ☐ No ☐   Knowledge of transportation planning techniques,
                applications and methods. Includes analysis of envi-
                ronmental impacts, land use patterns, employment
                projections, and effects on neighborhood planning.
                Includes development and evaluation of paratransit
                alternatives.

LAND USE ISSUES

Yes ☐ No ☐   Knowledge of various land use issues such as neigh-
                borhood planning, park siting and residential and
                industrial development. Includes the development and
                use of capital improvement programming, zoning and
                service boundaries. Includes identification of fund
                sources and environmental and economic impacts.

Yes ☐ No ☐   Skill in dealing effectively with the public. Distributing
                information, acting as an advocate, dealing with
                people in sensitive situations.

Yes ☐ No ☐   Skill in planning and coordinating work projects and
                processes. Includes establishing goals, time frames,
                alternatives and evaluative methods.

Yes ☐ No ☐   Skill in reading and interpreting maps and charts.
                Including topographical maps, plat maps, aerial
                photographs.

ECONOMICS

Yes ☐ No ☐   Knowledge of economic theory as applied to urban
                and regional planning. Includes application of location
                theory, the identification and analysis of industrial
                growth trends, analysis of site-specific economic
                conditions. Also includes interpretation and analysis
                of the economic impacts of various transportation,
                land use, population and employment developments.

POPULATION AND EMPLOYMENT FORECASTING

Yes ☐ No ☐   Skill in developing and analyzing demographic projec-
                tions for urban areas using cohort survival tables,
                adjusting secondary source forecasts to fit local condi-
                tions. Skill in applying demographic findings to plan-
                ning issues such as transportation housing and labor
                force forecasts, land use requirements and use of
                public facilities.

Source: Mary McFadyen, Personnel Analyst, City of Portland, Oregon, Civil Service
Board.

1. *We can reliably predict future manpower needs: Fact:* We cannot now predict future needs accurately enough for individuals to plan careers based on current advice. Such guides as the *Occupational Outlook Handbook* are out of date by the time they are published. (For example, the 1978 edition forecast an annual need for 1,100 additional planners. However, this was an extrapolation made before Proposition 13 in California and the budget cutting fever caught up with local government hiring.)

2. *Somewhere there is a system or institution which can be relied upon to link the job hunter with the job: Fact:* What exists is imperfect and does not function in the best interests of the job hunter. Eighty percent of all jobs paying more than $600 per month are not advertised through normal channels. These jobs are filled by personal contacts or by chance.

3. *The most effective tool for the job hunter is a good resume: Fact:* Resumes are people on paper, to be shuffled by personnel departments or executive secretaries, filed and forgotten. The most effective tool for the job hunter is the personal interview—talking persuasively and honestly to the person who has the power to hire him.

4. *The person who is chosen among many applicants is the person who is best qualified: Fact:* Often the person who knows the most about getting hired gets the job. Consider the problem of selecting the right person to hire from the employer's point of view. Would you choose solely on the basis of test scores, performance in school, and experience carefully composed for a resume? It is doubtful you would, particularly if you had many candidates. You would probably choose someone who demonstrated a clear understanding of your needs and presented himself or herself as the sort of person that could meet those needs. There is nothing self-evident about you and getting a job is work itself.

Step Three: Interviews

Theodore Novey said, the purpose of an interview is to find out about those things that the interviewee is probably afraid to tell. . . .Some of the important questions are:
How smart are you?
How independent are you?
Can you work and share authority and decisions with others?
What happens when you don't get your own way?
Can you make mistakes and take responsibility for them?
Do you work hard? How lazy are you?
How well do you understand the work that you propose to do?
Do you like yourself?
Do you like me? Can we enjoy working together?
What makes you angry?

What makes you frightened?
What are your strong points?
What are your weak points?
How much are you worth in salary?
What do you want from this job?
What do you want from me?
What happens when you are angry, scared or frustrated?[6]

Can you answer these questions for the person you'd like to work for? In addition to knowing answers to questions such as these, you should be able to express them confidently and smoothly.

Toni St. James, program coordinator for the California Employment Development Department, said:

> An interview is emotional, not intellectual. If the interviewer doesn't like you in the first 12 seconds, there is little chance he will like you 12 minutes later. Therefore, the primary purpose of a job interview is to make a strong first impression and maintain it. . .
>
> You've got to convince your employer that you are imaginative, perceptive, creative—yet you won't rock the boat. You've got to look him in the eye and give him your full body attention. Body language is crucial.
>
> And so is your voice. Keep it even, smooth. You will probably be asked questions meant to excite you, but take a deep breath and reply calmly. . .
>
> Remember, everyone who reaches the interview stage is already deemed qualified for the job. . .
>
> What you must do in the interview is make an impression that is solid and will last, and the only impressions that last are very good ones and very bad ones.''[7]

Some of the things usually covered in a governmental interview are depicted in the San Francisco Civil Service Commission rating sheet (see Figure 6.3) which was used until recently. The questions asked are meant not to gather facts so much as to get you to reveal yourself. To do this, stress questions such as the following are asked:

LEADING QUESTIONS. ''What do you think of the statement that planners (engineers, administrators, and so on) like doctors like to play God? What a question such as this is trying to uncover is how you'd handle statements from opinionated people at a public hearing or in the office. Answer calmly and reasonably. Humor is unfortunately considered flip by most interview panels. This author blew an interview in a well-known ''radical'' city by replying to this question, ''If it's God you've got an opening for, planners will assume the role cheaper than doctors.''

Figure 6.3. Qualifications Appraisal Rating Sheet

Examination(s): _____ Candidate: _____

RATING GUIDE (Check one for each category)	Unacceptable	Acceptable	Well-Qualified	Superior
In relation to position applied for:				
1. *General Impression:* Appearance, manner, poise	____	____	____	____
2. *Ability to Express Self:* Ability to understand questions and communicate responses effectively.	____	____	____	____
3. *Personal Development:* Evidence of reliability, stability, personal adjustment, ability to relate to others, tact, self-confidence, emotional maturity	____	____	____	____
4. *Education:* Consider in addition to minimum qualifications any special studies or pertinent training.	____	____	____	____
5. *Experience:* Length, pertinence of recency of experience, indications of progressively more responsible duties. Evidence that experience has been of particular benefit to candidate in relation to position.	____	____	____	____
6. *Supervision and/or Administration:* (To be rated only if required in this class. Indications of ability to effectively plan, organize, direct and control the work of others.	____	____	____	____

Other: (Specify)

For all evaluation: Considering all of the above factors and any other relevant qualifications which the candidate may possess or lack, how do you rate his suitability for this position? *Circle one numerical rating:*

Unacceptable: 65   *Acceptable:* 70-71-72-73-74-75-76-77-78-79   *Well-Qualified:* 80-81-82-83-84-85-86-87-88-89
Superior: 90-91-92-93-94-95-96-97-98-99-100

Notes: A rating of 65% must be documented on the reverse side to show the facts on which the rating was made. A rating which appears unusual in relation to a candidates education or experience qualifications should also be documented. A score of 65 made by a *majority* of board members is disqualifying. An average rating below 70% where a majority of the board rated the candidate as acceptable will be considered passing.

Signature _____ **Date** _____

Source: Civil Service Commission of San Francisco.

ZAPPING YOU PERSONALLY. "You've done a lot of skipping around from major to major and job to job. Why should we believe you'll change this pattern if you get this job?" Watch out! They are trying to find out how you react when someone pushes a personal button. Will you flare up into anger, hostility, freeze into silence, get defensive, or try to talk your way out—all of which may be fatal.

Stay cool. It's okay to disagree—but softly. For example, you might pause, think, and reply with something like, "Yes, I did move around a lot when I was a student, but I felt I needed to find diversity in training and experience. Now I'm more certain of what I can do and what I want, and this job seems to be a good fit for my abilities and work preferences.

QUESTIONS FOR WHICH THERE IS NO ANSWER. This is the trap laid for phonies and know-it-alls. It's okay to say you don't know to such questions. In fact, it's the only reasonable answer. You might answer some questions assertively and with finesse. For example, "If you become our Planner II, how would you do a social element for our city in three months?" You could say: "I don't know right now, but if I were hired, I'd be able to come back with an answer as to what would be feasible in a short time and how."

TELL US A LITTLE ABOUT YOURSELF. This is the most difficult test for many. It tests your poise, warmth, communication skills, imagination, judgment, and self-esteem. Tell them some of your pluses— I'm good at working alone without needing a lot of direction, but I can also work well in a team situation, where I often feel the most innovative. Finish, wait for questions, and then solicit them if you feel you haven't registered. Never recite your resume. They already have that; this is an occasion for you to show how well you think and communicate without props.

DOS AND DON'TS FOR INTERVIEWING
1. Know why you are taking the interview and want the job.
2. Know precisely what you can do on behalf of your employer.
3. Know how much you're going to cost.
4. A committee makes camels, not stallions. Don't permit them to turn you into one. Most of the time, interview panels and personnel people screen (eliminate) people. They don't choose them. So finishing in the money isn't good enough. Stay loose, be brief and clear. Don't fill in silences with sales talk. If you'd been looking at tense, eager strangers all day, you'd know that silence is golden.

5. Save your best shots and questions for the person who counts—the person who has the power to hire you.
6. Don't be negative. Don't, for example, bad mouth former employers to build yourself up as a morally superior person who had the character to quit the company of evil and incompetent people.
7. Don't act cocky, flip, or overconfident. Even if your human potential instructor told you you're perfect, you may strike your interviewers as so inner-directed that you'd be difficult to direct from the outside.
8. Don't accept a job on the spot (or reject one either). Think about what you're getting into. Sleep on it. Do any more questions come to mind? This is the time to see if there are any Catch 22s in the job (see Figure 6.4).
9. When you've got a firm offer, negotiate for the future, not just the present. Negotiate for the terms of your promotion now. Will you, for example, be promoted for doing a good job or will you have to surpass all comers in a civil service free-for-all job competition which stresses experience and skills unconnected to what you're doing on the job you accept. Know what success on the job means and where it can lead before you accept.

And when the negotiations are resolved, get it in writing if you can. In any case, know what you can and will do about it if the agreement made when they hired you isn't kept. Most government jobs, especially at the management level, are not unionized. You will be your own shop steward, grievance committee, and contract enforcer. In those cases where the boss or the agency is unfair, there are only three options open:

1. Hang in there, maybe things will change or you won't mind it so much when you get used to it.
2. Quit before the place does bad things to your head.
3. Adopt the classic bureaucratic defense by doing the very minimum amount of work allowable for this unfair place.

None of these options will be a growth experience, so it's always best to choose jobs wisely and carefully.

PREPARATION FOR AN INTERVIEW. Before you go to an interview, complete the self-evaluation (see Figure 6.5). Then think out the responses you are going to give to questions such as the following. Questions such as these may actually arise during an interview.

1. What are your long-term goals? What do you want to be doing ten years from now?
2. Why do you want to work for us? Why should we hire you?

Figure 6.4. Getting There is Half The Fun! (?)

A foolproof guide to taking an interview with a high class consulting firm if you don't speak Arabic or Persian or Fortran.

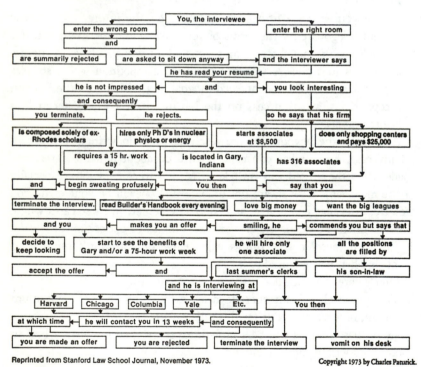

Reprinted from Stanford Law School Journal, November 1973.

3. What are your greatest strengths? Weaknesses?
4. Why do you think you are ready to take on the responsibilities of this job?
5. How long have you remained on previous jobs?
6. What are you looking for in this job?
7. What contribution can you make to our objectives? What can you do for us that someone else can't?

Figure 6.5. Self-Evaluation

Complete a form like this one that honestly describes you. In a job interview, sell the positive traits and neutralize the negatives.

Positive Traits	Negative Traits
1. I work well with others.	1. My experience is limited.
2. I am well organized.	2. I stutter and can't speak well before groups.
3. I am poised and personable.	
4. I have a good vocabulary and use it.	3. I have had limited management experience.
5. I write well.	4. I am a procrastinator.
6. I am self-motivated and can carry out tasks with a minimum of supervision.	5. Writing is difficult for me, and I don't do it very well.
	6. I loose my temper easily.
7.	7.
8.	8.

8. What are the three most important accomplishments thus far in your career?

9. Do you work well under pressure?

10. What other than working here do you want to do with your life? What are your interests, hobbies, and so on?

11. Are you willing to work hard, evenings, and some weekends?

12. List your skills (vocational and avocational).

13. What skills do you wish you had that you don't now have?

14. What are you going to do about increasing your skills bank?

15. What is your attitude about belonging to a professional society?

16. What experiences have you had in supervising others?

17. What positions are you considering?

18. Did you enjoy your last job? If yes, why are you leaving? If not, why not?

19. Does your present employer know you are looking for another job?

20. What salary are you worth?

21. What salary are you willing to work for?

22. What did you like best (or least) about your last employer?

23. Do you intend to carry on any outside work?

24. Have you ever been fired or refused a promotion?

25. Do you prefer working with others or working alone?

26. Are you active in outside groups or organizations?

27. How many hours per week do you think a person should spend on the job?

28. What do you think of attending meetings?

29. If someone called you a name in a public meeting, how would you handle the situation?
30. What is your attitude about the employer-employee relationship in arriving at decisions?
31. Do you consider yourself success oriented?
32. What is the most rewarding assignment you have ever completed?
33. Are you innovative? Explain.
34. Are you competitive? Explain.

Remember, some of these questions might put you on the defensive. The interviewer may not care as much about the answer as how you respond. Are you cool or do you panic? Employers want to be sure you are worth hiring. They don't want any surprises later, and a good interviewer can use many facts in arriving at the conclusion: Should I hire this person, or will I be sorry later if I do?

SUMMARY

1. List skills you've had a long time and feel confident about.
2. List skills you've recently acquired.
3. List skills you most enjoy using (some of 1 plus 2).
4. List where you want to work (in a public agency, with a consultant, advocacy group, and so on).
5. List job types or tasks you would like to undertake (even if you're not sure you're totally ready for them yet).
6. List the skills you want to develop so that you can perform better on your current or next position.
7. Write a draft resume.
8. Test the resume on your friends, both those who know something about you and those who do not.
9. Revise the resume and prepare it in final form.
10. Go job hunting.
11. If selected for an interview, be prepared to answer basic questions about your experience, education, values, life goals, and skills. Be prepared to answer the most basic questions of all, which may be asked directly or "hidden" in these two basic questions: "What can you do for us?" and "Why should I hire you?" How will you answer if you don't know something about yourself and about the agency or firm interviewing you? Find out before the interview. And ask your own

questions at the interview. Interview the interviewer. Then orient your answers to their needs while also cogently and persuasively describing and selling your skills and other attributes. Do not assume your resume will do this job for you. All it does is get you in to the interview.

NOTES

1. Diane K. Shah, "What Does it Take to Make You Happy at Your Work?" Reprinted by permission of *The National Observer.* ©Dow Jones & Company, 1977. All Rights Reserved.

2. Richard Nelson Bolles, *What Color Is Your Parachute? A Practical Guide for Job-Hunters and Career-Changers* (Berkeley, California: Ten Speed Press, 1972), p. 133.

3. Bolles *(What Color Is Your Parachute?)* has a relevant observation: "You must identify the man or woman who has the power to hire you and show them how your skills can help them with their problems."

4. It also implies that, with tight budgets, CETA "cheap help" for local government, and program cutbacks, the University Ph.D's who always assumed that on-the-job training would be available for their unskilled graduates will have to restructure much of their course offerings if future graduates are going to find jobs. This, in turn, could cause some unemployment among more than a few tenured mandarins, which might also be a good thing, for then they would have to acquire useful skills themselves.

5. Julie Monson, "In the Meantime: A Strategy for Job Hunters," *Pomona Today* (Pomona College alumni magazine), March 1975, p. 7.

6. Theodore B. Novey, *T.A. for Management: Making Life Work* (Sacramento, California: Jalmar Press, 1976), p. 53.

7. Joseph Torchia, "How a Good First Impression Can Clinch a Job," *San Francisco Chronicle.* Reprinted with permission of the Chronicle Publishing Co., © 1978.

Chapter Seven
Growing With the Flow

You've heard of people calling in sick.
You may have called in sick a few times
yourself. But have you ever thought
about calling in well? It'd go like this:
you'd get the boss on the line and say,
"Listen, I've been sick ever since I
started working here, but today I'm well
and I won't be in anymore."

—Tom Robbins, *Even Cowgirls*
*Get the Blues**

Now that you've been hired and have been on the job for a while—and it's wise to stay put for at least one year—you may want to take stock of your situation, reassess your job and your career plan, and decide what to do next.

TAKING STOCK OF YOUR SITUATION

No one formula for career planning and development works for everyone. This absence of surefire techniques need not discourage you, however. Bear in mind that your particular needs are individual and specific and will depend on what you already know, what skills you want to learn, and where you see yourself going.

First, you need to accept the notion that there is not room for everyone at the top. Not only are a lot of people employed in middle management, but they are needed there. If you do not aspire to be the chief executive officer (CEO), you should not allow yourself to be targeted into the kinds of situations where becoming a supervisor and then the boss is inevitable.

*Boston: Houghton Mifflin Company, 1976, p. 73.

Decide what is right for you and then place the job of career planning and development in your own hands. Using the self-analysis in chapter 6 should help (see Figure 6.5).

Second, size up your job from two viewpoints: (1) What can you contribute to it, and (2) what can it contribute to your growth. Peter Drucker says: "If you are in a position where you have gotten as much out of the job, the boss and the company as you can get, if you are still below late middle age and have given all you are likely to give, then it is time to move on. However, don't rush. Keep in mind that a person moves out because of success as much as failure."[1] In short, are you maximizing your opportunities by staying or by moving on? If by staying, what do you have to do to counteract or deal with obsolescence, to function more effectively, to ensure that the boss will acknowledge your performance and value indefinitely?

Some of us need to define those things which most directly affect our ability to function effectively on our current jobs and to determine what we need to do our present jobs better. Others need to define those things which are most likely to ensure being in the right place at the right time, that is, being ready for a new opportunity when it arises.

Do You Have the Right Kind of Intelligence for the Job You Are Doing?

Addison Steele, in his book *Upward Nobility,* argues that asking philosophical questions is painful, maybe even foolish, and that the brightest people, even the most knowledgeable, are least likely to secure positions of great power in corporations.[2] Probably these conclusions hold true within the public sector, too. The "wrong kind of intelligence," he says, "makes you ask 'profound questions' such as: 'Am I truly happy? Does my life have meaning? Is what I am doing important?'" Steele says chances are that the five most powerful people in any large company have never asked themselves these questions because they don't have the inclination.

What about you? Do you suppress or do you ask such questions? The ones who ask often abandon their careers to raise grapes in the Napa Valley or make furniture in Vermont. It may mean that too much intelligence or unbridled philosophical and thoughtful inclinations are handicaps. You may have to work in an atmosphere where you, and all of the smartest people, do not make the major decisions. This is an immensely frustrating circumstance. Even more so if they look at you—and at knowledge, and new ideas, and new ways of looking at things—as overrated commodities. (But, isn't that why they hired you, you say?)

So, if you want to get ahead, be prepared to develop the proven qualities of success: motivation, high energy, self-confidence, and a single-mindedness about getting to a goal on time no matter what. You may be smart, have intelligence and splendid credentials, but having the "basic" attributes of drive and determination seems to count most of all.

I Enjoy My Job and Frankly Don't Want to Take the Next Step Up the Ladder

Well, who says you must make it to the top? Many people who move up the success ladder do it because it's the right thing for them to do. They like the upward mobility, new responsibilities, prestige, power, and money. And they are secure and competent enough to do what is expected of them. But, if you enjoy your present job and it's stimulating, or maybe you travel a lot and meet interesting people, or just stay in the office which is comfortable for you, or if you don't want to take on new responsibilities, you may not want to head toward the top. That is fine. The choice is yours.

The Keys to Advancement

The keys to advancement in public administration and planning are many; the most essential are basic knowledge, the right kind of intelligence, and the right collection of skills.

Some additional keys to success for a good public servant should entail the following:
1. Know how to get things done.
2. Understand the trade-offs that must be considered in the making of policies and their implementation.
3. Be familiar with current laws and legal opinions as well as current government programs and revenue sources.
4. Be able to appraise what he or she needs to know to grow on the job and where to get that knowledge.

These keys to success apply to everyone, those going to the top and those whose career is aimed at staying in middle management.

What Do You Personally Want Most from Your Career?

Each public service employee ought to complete a personal profile once in a while. This exercise obliges you to face up to the aspects of your work you like and to those you don't. If there are too many don'ts, maybe you're ready for a change.

So what do *you* personally want most from your career or job? Rate the following in order of importance (feel free to add other goals to this list):

1. A sense of accomplishment and achievement.
2. A chance to be creative.
3. Excitement.
4. High salary.
5. Prestige and peer reputation.
6. Freedom from normal employer-employee constraints (autonomy).
7. Friendships.
8. Intellectual stimulation.
9. A chance to serve others.
10. A chance to gain power.
11. A chance to influence others.
12. A chance to change public policy or processes to my liking.
13. A chance to develop skills.
14. Variety.
15. Leadership potential.
16. Meaningful work.

Now, what do you try hardest to avoid in your work?
1. Boredom.
2. Failure.
3. Foolishness and incompetence among peers.
4. Frustration.
5. Hard work.
6. Appearing in public.
7. Writing reports.
8. Research.
9. Working with data.
10. Graphics.
11. Loneliness.
12. Stress.
13. Surprises on the job.
14. Wasting time.

What You Can Do to Help Yourself

The chief lesson to be learned in the process of building a career is that you must manage your own. You must be active in influencing decisions made about you, and you need to recognize that good effort and performance alone is not necessarily rewarded. Modesty is not necessarily a virtue.

Before looking for another position, rigorously assess your strengths and weaknesses, what you like and don't like. Don't be trapped by formal, narrow descriptions about what you have a potential to do. Consider what you have learned and must still learn. The opportunity to develop should be universal. Developmental opportunities can be beneficial to most employees and to their organizations, and the resources should be there and be fairly and equitably distributed. American business executives know this. In 1976 *Business Week* estimated that at least 1 million already-employed men and women were boning up on business subjects through full-time or part-time courses.[3] Virtually all hoped that extra schooling would give them a leg up the executive ladder or would mean the critical difference between keeping or losing an executive position or new job. "For most students," *Business Week* said, "the real benefits seem to come less from the classroom drill than from the exposure to new ideas and the chance to compare notes with highly motivated peers." The student's companies typically footed the bill.

Federal agencies are leaning in the same direction, for they, too, want to nip obsolescence in the bud, give their employees educational opportunities that are likely to improve performance, and cause personnel, especially at the top- and middle-management levels, to learn new skills. One of the best examples is the Federal Executive Seminars sponsored by the U.S. Civil Service Commission. Other agencies that have been known to provide well for training in the face of rapidly changing techniques for environmental management are the Environmental Protection Agency (EPA) and the Forest Service.

However, it doesn't seem that the necessity for these kinds of efforts has been built into popular and political expectations at the state and especially the local levels. Clearly the evidence shows that the continuing education of local government employees has never risen high on the list of management priorities and is assured no protection from periodic budget-cutting sprees. So, it cannot be expected that breadth of knowledge and intellectual development will soon be recognized as important. Quantifiable and how-to-do-it-oriented training is still more easily defended than is the kind of intellectual growth and reorientation needed on a continuing basis in order to prevent personal, professional, and institutional obsolescence. Popular attacks on local government performances seem to ignore this reality, leaving the gap between the enlightened business and the public sector as wide as ever.

But there are some hints about what you can do to help yourself.

1. Have fun in your career and on the job. When you're no longer having fun, you're in need of a change.

2. Keep your sense of humor; much of what you put up with may be absurd. Being earnest and a true believer may have got you into the field but a sense of humor may do a lot to keep you there. Often bureaucratic idiocy is temporary, so it will help to keep the following Army motto firmly in mind: "This too shall pass."

3. Take positive steps to achieve your career objectives—through job enrichment, job changes, sabbaticals, continuing education, and travel. Prepare a career plan for yourself and stick to it.

4. Maintain your integrity as a special person with unique attributes, capabilities, and skills, Build on the best of each of these.

5. Remember the cardinal rule of public service: above all else ask who stands to profit and who to lose by virtue of the recommendations, decisions, or actions you initiate. Once you know the answer, be able to apply a standard of morality, fairness, and equitability that will stand the test of close scrutiny. If you find yourself losing sight of this

rule, it's probably time for rest, a new job, a career change, or early retirement.

6. Remember that public employment is a serious and useful business, but that not all of us know that. Your job must include ways to continually justify your employment and your service to your client. You must at all times expand the understanding and appreciation of the people around you concerning your role and purpose. If you aren't doing so, you may be ready to go out to pasture.

7. Surviving in the bureaucracy is a skill most of us learn while on the job. Since it's a form of self-preservation, we learn to survive while remaining effective and productive, and true to our values. Others metamorphosize into a true bureaucrat without knowing, and even their friends won't tell them. Then the coffee break and covering up become more important than the real work we are asked to do. Growing with the flow means knowing how to work within the bureaucracy without adopting too many of the bureaucracy's shortcomings.

8. Focus your attention on improving your management skills above all else. This makes sense even if you don't expect to become a manager. You will better be able to ''manage'' yourself and your own work, and maybe even those who supervise you. Subjects most continuing education schools offer that can help you are
   - management principles
   - time management
   - how to cope with difficult people
   - oral presentations and speaking in public
   - creative problem-solving techniques
   - executive effectiveness
   - organizational development and design
   - making the transition to a supervisory position
   - learning how to delegate authority and work.

9. Try to define those things which most directly affect your ability to function effectively on your current job, and determine what you need to do to do your present job better. Then make a logical decision about the purpose of acquiring new skills (avoiding those you cannot use) and determine which ones are appropriate for you. Only then is it time to look for a new job, if that is what you want. Putting it another way, if you feel stuck in a box on the organizational chart with no place to go, or find you don't want to advance to the next logical place, set down in writing those aspects of the job, the functions you perform which you like and perform well. What skills and working conditions

should prevail to make your job more fun, more useful, and more productive? If you were to acquire new skills, what would they be? What would you gain by having these new skills? Acquire the skills you need and want, and then go after the job you want.

When to Quit

If you've ever thought about quitting, it's usually for one of the following reasons:

1. You've been passed over for a promotion and you're humiliated, demoralized, or both; or there simply is no room higher up in the agency. It's time to get out of the "box" in which you find yourself.
2. The work you are doing is dull or not fulfilling, there are no prospects for better work, and you feel a need to seek out a new opportunity. (The best advice we can give you, given one or the other of these two circumstances, is don't quit too soon. Consider keeping your present job while you look for another. This strategy continues your income and your security. It also demonstrates to a prospective employer that you are making the job change voluntarily.)
3. A transfer to a new job may make sense because there's an opportunity to learn more, do more, and make more.
4. You want to retire, drop out, travel, go back to school, and so on.
5. An ethical or moral issue arises and the only honorable way out is to quit. Perhaps, "whistle blowing" is not appropriate, or nothing can be done to restore truth, honesty, or integrity where it is wanting. Raising a fuss isn't likely to do any good either. You decide either to get out gracefully or to write a letter of resignation blasting those you hold responsible for your dilemma or what you see wrong. Often such actions are markedly cathartic while making no significant impact on the agency and the behavior of those you hold responsible. Administrators have been known to quit when they concluded that the board was acting irresponsibly or dishonorably, or paying no attention. In any case, quitting on a matter of principle cannot be taken lightly, and yet it may be precisely the right thing to do under certain circumstances

Quitting and changing jobs is nothing to feel awkward about. Quitting can and should be a creative act under many circumstances. A job move may be just a link in a chain of job changes. According to the U.S. Department of Labor the hypothetical average person in his or her early

20s can expect to make more than six job changes during the remainder of a working life, at age 40 more than two, and at age 50, you can look forward to at least one more job change. While the holding power of fringe benefits, pensions, and seniority rights is enormous, professional and executive job changes and dropouts are commonplace. For those of you who may want to start a new career at midlife, make another career plan. Note the number of skills you possess. Undoubtedly, they are marketable if you know how to sell them and yourself and how to show a prospective employer how your education, experience, and your bank of skills can help him or her.

NOTES

1. "How to Boss the Boss—and Succeed," *San Francisco Chronicle*, June 8, 1977.

2. Addison Steele, *Upward Nobility: How to Win the Rat Race Without Becoming a Rat* (New York: Times Books, 1978), p. 133.

3. *Business Week*, March 8, 1976.

Bibliography

Bolles, Richard N. *What Color Is Your Parachute?* 5th rev. ed. Berkeley, California: Ten Speed Press, 1979.

This is a very practical manual for both job hunters and career changers.

Drucker, Peter. *The Effective Executive.* New York: Harper & Row, 1976.

The principles of effectiveness and good decisionmaking are laid out simply by one of the giants of management practice and theory.

Fox, Marcia R. *Put Your Degree to Work: Job-Hunting Success for the New Professional.* New York: W. W. Norton, 1979.

Workable guidelines are presented on career planning, the job search, resumes, and interviews. Examples and specific instructions on how to do these right are included.

Irish, Richard K. *Go Hire Yourself an Employer.* New York: Anchor Press, 1978.

This book tells how to organize your own luck in job hunting. It helps to alert job seekers to the deception sometimes found in newspaper want ads resulting from such things as affirmative action evasions.

McCay, James T. *The Management of Time.* Englewood Cliffs, N.J.: Prentice-Hall, 1959.

Methods of overcoming time pressures are related to increased personal growth.

McGregor, Douglas. *The Human Side of Enterprise.* New York: McGraw–Hill, 1960.

This is a classic study on humanely managing subordinates.

Radovic, Igor D. *How to Manage the Boss: The Radovic Rule.* New York: M. Evans, 1973.

How to win by subordination rather than insubordination is discussed in this humorous book.

Taetzsch, Lyn, and Benson, Eileen. *Taking Charge on the Job: Techniques for Assertive Management.* New York: Executive Enterprises, 1978.

The authors advance ideas on techniques that can help employees become effective and productive managers. A variety of interpersonal situations where people learn to listen effectively, handle criticism, and be assertive are described.

Tarrant, John J. *Getting Fired: An American Ordeal.* New York: Van Nostrand Reinhold, 1975.

Tarrant discusses how to cope with the peculiarly American tension of prospective dismissal, the shock of getting fired, and how to recover income and self-esteem afterward.

Warren W. Jones has worked as a city planner in California since 1956 and since 1972 has chaired the program in Continuing Education in Environmental Design at the University of California, Berkeley. **Albert Solnit**, a city planner, architect, and economist, lives in Portland, Oregon, but has practiced and taught planning throughout the country and abroad. He is the author of *The Job of the Planning Commissioner*. Both men have conducted courses on career development.

Also available from APA's Planners Press

The Citizen's Guide to Planning. Herbert H. Smith. 2nd ed., revised and expanded. 1979. 208 pp. $7.95 (paperback); $6.50 each for 10 or more copies. An excellent comprehensive introduction to planning for the layman and aspiring professional alike.

City Zoning. Clifford L. Weaver and Richard F. Babcock. 1980. 328 pp. $16.95 (paperback); APA members and PAS subscribers $14.95. An important book on how cities are using zoning to revive the urban core.

Order from
American Planning Association
1313 E. 60th St.
Chicago, IL 60637